THE MYSTERY OF LIFE

HOW NOTHING BECAME EVERYTHING

THE MYSTERY OF LIFE

JAN PAUL SCHUTTEN

ILLUSTRATED BY FLOOR RIEDER

ALADDIN
New York London Toronto Sydney New Delhi

BEYOND WORDS
Hillsboro, Oregon

ALADDIN
An imprint of Simon & Schuster
Children's Publishing Division
1230 Avenue of the Americas
New York, NY 10020

BEYOND WORDS
20827 N.W. Cornell Road, Suite 500
Hillsboro, Oregon 97124-9808
503-531-8700 / 503-531-8773 fax
www.beyondword.com

This Beyond Words/Aladdin edition September 2015
Text copyright © 2013 by Jan Paul Schutten
Interior illustrations copyright © 2013 by Floor Rieder
English language translation copyright © 2015 by Laura Watkinson
This title was previously published in Dutch as *Het Raadsel Van Alles Wat Leeft* in 2013 in the Netherlands by Uitgeverij J.H. Gottmer
Cover copyright © 2015 by Beyond Words (cover artwork/font set in Critter)

For information about special discounts for bulk purchases, please contact Simon & Schuster Special Sales at 1-866-506-1949 or business@simonandschuster.com.

The Simon & Schuster Speakers Bureau can bring authors to your live event. For more information or to book an event, contact the Simon & Schuster Speakers Bureau at 1-866-248-3049 or visit our website at www.simonspeakers.com.

Managing Editor: Lindsay S. Brown
Editor: Nicole Geiger
Copyeditors: Kristin Thiel, Emmalisa Sparrow
Design: Sara E. Blum
The text of this book was set in Adobe Caslon Pro and Interstate.

Manufactured in China 0615 SCP

10 9 8 7 6 5 4 3 2 1

Nederlands
letterenfonds
dutch foundation
for literature
This book was published with the support of the Dutch Foundation for Literature

Library of Congress Cataloging-in-Publication Data

Schutten, Jan Paul.
 [Raadsel van alles wat leeft. English]
 The mystery of life : how nothing became everything / Jan Paul Schutten ; illustrated by Floor Rieder ; translated by Laura Watkinson.
  pages cm
 "Originally published in Dutch. Gottmer Uitgevers Groep 2013."
 Audience: Ages 10-14.
 Includes bibliographical references and index.
 1. Life (Biology)—Juvenile literature. 2. Life—Origin—Juvenile literature. 3. Evolution—Juvenile literature. 4. Discoveries in science—Juvenile literature. I. Rieder, Floor, illustrator. II. Watkinson, Laura, translator. III. Title.
 QH501.S3813 2015
 576—dc23
                                                    2014039916

ISBN 978-1-58270-525-5 (paper over board)
ISBN 978-1-4814-2918-4 (eBook)

CONTENTS

FOREWORD

For around 4 billion years, a horribly hot planet calmly did its laps around the sun, sizzling and bubbling. Then something really weird happened. Right in the midst of all that boiling and hissing, life began. Just like that. No one knows exactly how. But we know what the results were. All sorts of microscopic offspring soon covered the planet in purple, yellow, and white blobs of slime. In tepid pools and along the shores of the seas and in small cavities in the solidified lava from volcanoes . . . this living slime could grow everywhere. The smell must have been terrible, like sulfur and rotten eggs, and the stench of farts and stinky socks. But gradually other living things began to develop from that slime: worms and slugs, fungi and algae. And the surface of our planet, which we call Earth, has been teeming with all kinds of life ever since.

Four billion years after life first began in the form of bacteria, humans now walk around on our planet. Humans are animals, but we're animals of a very special kind. We're the only animals that can ponder tricky questions: Which socks should I wear today? What will the weather be like tomorrow? Why is water so wet? Where does life come from? And what about all these animals and plants? Where did they come from? And how about humans? It's often children who ask these kinds of questions (adults are much more likely to think: *Yeah, right, whatever*). Children are curious. They want to know about all kinds of things. But fortunately some adults are curious too.

They become scientists and try to find out why everything is the way it is. A physicist can explain why water is wet. A biologist can tell us why a worm is alive and a stone is not, or why farts smell so bad. And a paleontologist can work out exactly how huge a tyrannosaurus's hind leg was. That's how we come to understand more and more about how the world works. We now have a fairly accurate idea of how old the universe is and how old the Earth is, how animals and plants developed over the course of millions of years, and why the cow and the whale are more closely related than the cow and the horse.

But how to explain it all? Scientists are good at investigating all kinds of tricky questions, but explaining something tricky is a different job altogether. You need a journalist to do that, or a writer: someone like Jan Paul Schutten. He's very good indeed at explaining complicated concepts. In this book, he explains such a huge number of things that you might need to read it a few times before you understand it all. Even more important, he also says that there are things we *don't* yet know. We still don't get how the very first life began. Did it just happen spontaneously? Did it come hurtling out of space? Was it actually created by a god? There's still room for doubt about some scientific questions. Remaining curious and full of new questions is what makes science so much fun. What's beyond the end of the universe? How many more years will the sun last? If birds are dinosaurs, is it really true that dinosaurs are extinct? Where was the first modern human being born? And how can learning about science be this much fun?

—Jelle Reumer, director, Natural History Museum, Rotterdam

JUST A QUICK WORD BEFORE WE REALLY GET STARTED

This book has some absolutely huge numbers in it. Numbers that are so big they're hard to imagine. For example, *Tiktaalik roseae*, one of the heroes of this book, lived around 370 million years ago. You have 86 billion[1] brain cells. And there are trillions of bacteria in your body. But what does that really mean? The following chart expresses those numbers in terms of time, to give you an idea of just how big all those millions, billions, and trillions actually are.

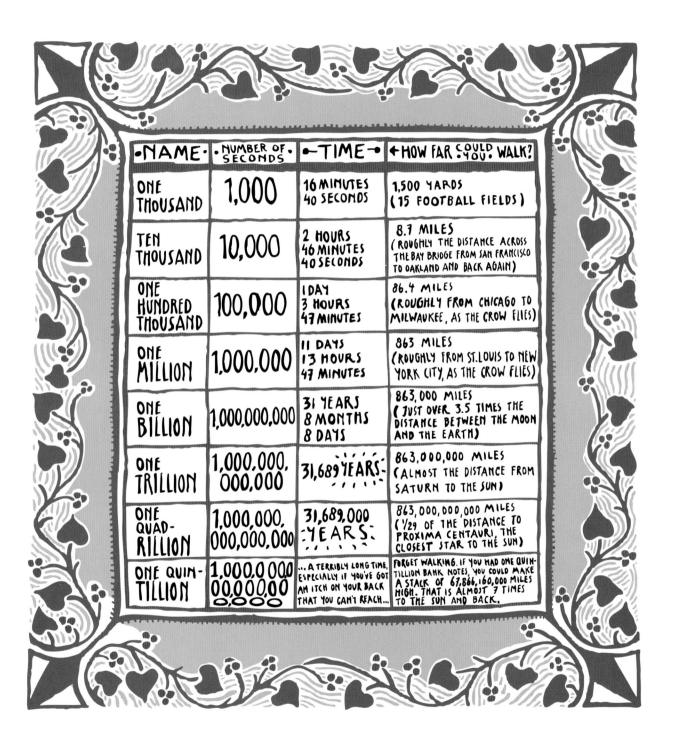

•NAME•	NUMBER OF SECONDS	←TIME→	←HOW FAR COULD YOU WALK?
ONE THOUSAND	1,000	16 MINUTES 40 SECONDS	1,500 YARDS (15 FOOTBALL FIELDS)
TEN THOUSAND	10,000	2 HOURS 46 MINUTES 40 SECONDS	8.7 MILES (ROUGHLY THE DISTANCE ACROSS THE BAY BRIDGE FROM SAN FRANCISCO TO OAKLAND AND BACK AGAIN)
ONE HUNDRED THOUSAND	100,000	1 DAY 3 HOURS 47 MINUTES	86.4 MILES (ROUGHLY FROM CHICAGO TO MILWAUKEE, AS THE CROW FLIES)
ONE MILLION	1,000,000	11 DAYS 13 HOURS 47 MINUTES	863 MILES (ROUGHLY FROM ST. LOUIS TO NEW YORK CITY, AS THE CROW FLIES)
ONE BILLION	1,000,000,000	31 YEARS 8 MONTHS 8 DAYS	863,000 MILES (JUST OVER 3.5 TIMES THE DISTANCE BETWEEN THE MOON AND THE EARTH)
ONE TRILLION	1,000,000, 000,000	31,689 YEARS	863,000,000 MILES (ALMOST THE DISTANCE FROM SATURN TO THE SUN)
ONE QUAD-RILLION	1,000,000, 000,000,000	31,689,000 YEARS	863,000,000,000 MILES (1/29 OF THE DISTANCE TO PROXIMA CENTAURI, THE CLOSEST STAR TO THE SUN)
ONE QUIN-TILLION	1,000,0000 00,00000 0,000	...A TERRIBLY LONG TIME, ESPECIALLY IF YOU'VE GOT AN ITCH ON YOUR BACK THAT YOU CAN'T REACH...	FORGET WALKING. IF YOU HAD ONE QUIN-TILLION BANK NOTES, YOU COULD MAKE A STACK OF 67,866,160,000 MILES HIGH. THAT IS ALMOST 7 TIMES TO THE SUN AND BACK.

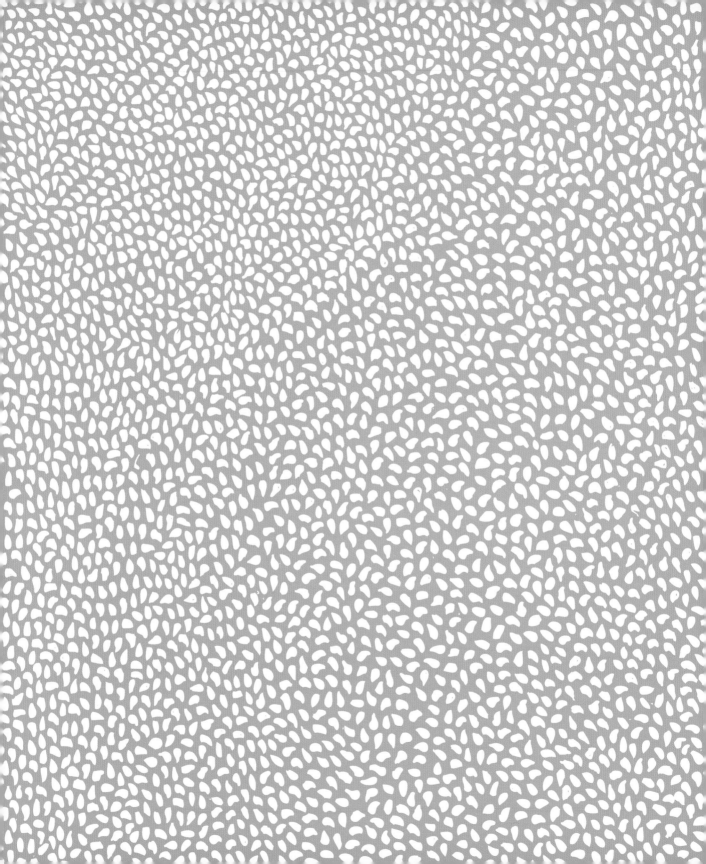

CHAPTER 1

Marvels, Mysteries, and You

Let's just take a moment to applaud the slipper animalcule! *Who? What?* The slipper animalcule, also known as the paramecium, is a tiny creature that's smaller than the dot on this *i*. *But why should we celebrate it? What's so special about it?* This tiny little thing deserves a huge round of applause simply for being alive. That's more of an achievement than you might think! And I'm going to tell you why.

Danish professor Henrik Schärfe has created a robot version[1] of himself. When the professor and his robot are together, people have to look twice to tell which one is the person and which one is the machine. The robot can't do very much at the moment. It can move a bit, but what it does best is look like its creator. It can't do anything else. Not even talk. But I'll eat a whole

sack full of rabbit food if someone, at some point in the future, doesn't design a robot that looks just like a person, that can give intelligent answers to your questions, and that can even play soccer with you. In fact, I think we'll be smart enough to build one within 30 years. But making a slipper animalcule? That task is thousands of times trickier.

The tiny paramecium can't do very much. It can swim a bit, doing the breaststroke with its minuscule hairs. It can drink dirty ditchwater and munch on the bacteria that are in the water. It can pee the water back out again. Well, it's more like sweating than peeing. It can mate with another slipper animalcule. It can divide itself in two so that there are suddenly two slipper animalcules instead of one. What else can it do? Um . . . almost nothing at all.

The slipper animalcule might be capable of doing less than Professor Schärfe's robot, but it can do one thing that a machine will never be able

R.I.P.
— SLIPPER —
ANIMALCULE
2.18.2015
✝ 2.20.2015
"I HAD TWO
AWESOME
DAYS!"

to: it can die. Of course, a robot can break, but that's different. We can often repair something that's broken, but we can never bring something back to life after it's died. Life is very special, even though quintillions of creatures have already lived on Earth.

The slipper animalcule is alive, and a robot isn't—that's the biggest difference. But there are also similarities. One of those similarities is that they're both made from lifeless things. Everything you see—and everything you can't see—is made of atoms and molecules. These are very, very small building blocks that make up everything in the universe, from slipper animalcules to trees, stars, planets, sacks of rabbit food, cucumbers, Joe Schmo from Buffalo's stinky socks, clouds, cream puffs, and robots. Yes, even Lady Gaga is made up of atoms. And all of those atoms are completely lifeless.

There's as much life in them as a brick, a heap of clay, or a Lego brick. So how can life come from all those lifeless atoms? How did life on Earth begin? Where do slipper animalcules come from? Where do we human beings come from? Is it possible that other life-forms exist in the universe? You can read about all of these subjects in this book.

SIMPLE CELLS?

The slipper animalcule is a very simple creature. It consists of one single cell. Just as everything around us is made from atoms, everything that is alive is also made up of cells. And, of course, those cells are in turn made of atoms. But while the atoms are as lifeless as a Lego brick, the cells are bursting with life, as you can see when you study them through a microscope: everything is all swirling and sloshing around. If you could shrink yourself and step inside a cell, you'd want to jump straight back out again. It's like a highway at rush hour, a log flume, a tornado, and a snowball fight, all wrapped up together.

How Many Cells Are There in You?

A cell's made up of more parts than 20 of Professor Schärfe's robots combined. And yet a cell's so small that it's impossible to see it with the naked eye. So if you can see a living creature, you know it has to be made up of a lot more cells than one. How many? Why don't we take you as an example? You're made up of, um, let me think . . . two, three, five, eight, nine, no . . . yes . . . 37.2 trillion cells. Thirty-seven point two trillion![2] And you really, really, really need them.

In the time it takes you to read just this one sentence, around 10 million new red blood cells have formed in your body. They're like tiny trucks that transport oxygen to the farthest reaches of your body. Without that

37,200,000,000,000

oxygen, other cells in your body would die. But you've got trillions of cells in your gut alone. All together, they cover a surface area as big as a tennis court. They're responsible for converting your food into fuel for your body. Without that fuel, you'd keel over and die. Or what about the cells that make up your heart? Your heart is a muscle that never grows tired. It beats every second, every minute, every day, year in, year out, without interruption, pumping blood through blood vessels with a combined length that goes twice around the world.

Cells are alive. That means they can die. Luckily, you also have cells that can clear away the dead cells and dispose of them. If you don't dust and clean your bedroom for a while, you'll see some of those dead cells. A lot of the dust in your home is dead skin cells. You lose about 30,000 of them every minute. Nine pounds a year. Within just a few weeks, all of your old skin cells have been replaced by new ones.[3]

So, What's Going on inside Your Body?

There's a lot happening inside your body. I've mentioned just a couple of things, but in reality there are a few million. Per second. All of those events inside your body are controlled by your brain. The brain is made up of around 86 billion brain cells.[4] They make your head a supercomputer that lets you do things that all the computers in the world couldn't do, even if they all

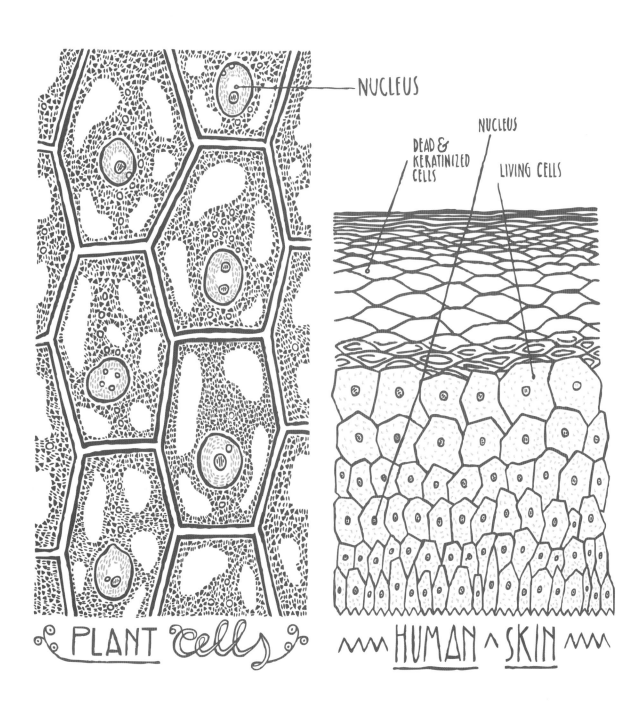

NUCLEUS

DEAD & KERATINIZED CELLS

NUCLEUS

LIVING CELLS

PLANT Cells

HUMAN ^ SKIN

worked together. Like the air traffic control tower at an airport, the brain cells make sure all of the other cells in your body do what they're supposed to do. They're the most important and complex cells that you have.

Is all of this starting to make your head spin? Good. That is the idea. You don't have to remember all these numbers, though. You don't even need to understand them. I only mentioned them to show you just how incredibly complicated your body is. The individual cells are special enough, but when they all work together in your body, they really are quite amazing. That's because they're the building blocks that make up you: a thinking, moving, talking, reading, laughing marvel.

Hey, if you gave the slipper animalcule a round of applause, you can give yourself a big hand now too. Go on!

MINUSCULE MARVELS

You are a marvel, the slipper animalcule is a marvel, and Joe Schmo from Buffalo's stinky socks are a marvel—well, actually, not the socks themselves, but the bacteria that live in them. That's because every single living thing is a marvel. Think about it. Can you make something living out of something that's lifeless? Can you make a living plant out of Lego bricks, for example? No, of course you can't.

Atoms are every bit as lifeless as Lego bricks, but for millions of years, this planet has been teeming with life, all of which is made up of those lifeless atoms. That's a marvel, isn't it? But it gets even crazier. You might think I wrote this book all on my own. That's only half true. Because I have about three-and-a-half pounds of bacteria in my body,[5] without whom this book would never have been created. Because if those little critters weren't there, I'd die very quickly. The bacteria convert the food in my intestines into energy and break down substances. Everything that's left over has to be expelled from my body. So they're very useful. That's why you've got a whole load of them too. There are millions of them just on the tip of your nose and on the end of your big toe as well, just as there are on every other square inch of your skin. But most of them are inside your body.

What Do Bacteria Look Like?

Those bacteria have been there since you were born. You already had some inside of you when you came out of your mom's tummy, but the most important ones entered your body with her milk.[6] They soon created a sizeable colony, and you've had these tiny companions inside your body ever since. Always in exactly the right quantities, too, unless you're sick. So you're never alone. Would you like me to introduce you to your inhabitants?

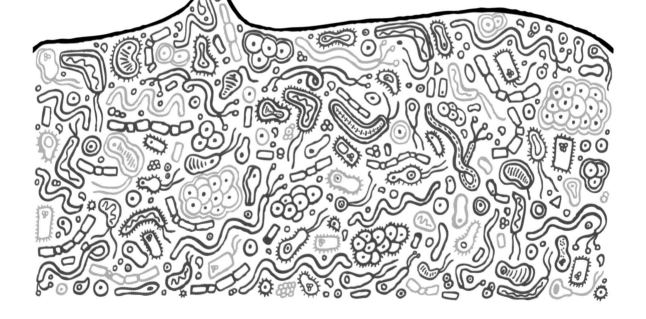

The slipper animalcule is already pretty small, but bacteria are even smaller and punier. That's why they appear on the slipper animalcule's dinner menu. Bacteria come in all kinds of shapes: round, spiral, like a rod, in the shape of a comma or a bunch of grapes, and with and without a tail. That "tail" is called a flagellum, which is Latin for "whip," and they can whirl it around 100,000 times a minute. It's like a kind of motor that they use to propel themselves forward. But a flagellum is way more complicated than an engine built by humans. Even such minuscule creatures have a smarter design than anything the biggest brains at a university could devise.

What Do Bacteria Taste Like?

Bacteria can be found all over our planet, and they've been there ever since the very beginning of life on Earth. They're the most successful living creatures. Wherever you look, they're there. But you can't see them, unless there are billions of them bunched together. You can taste them, though: there are plenty of bacteria in sauerkraut, yogurt, and spoiled milk. They're to blame for the sour taste. In fact, there are so many bacteria out there that it's difficult *not* to come across them.

Good bacteria keep you alive, but having the wrong bacteria in your body can prove fatal. That's why operating rooms have to be cleaned very carefully and doctors wear special antibacterial clothing. If they wore their scrubs to eat a sandwich in the cafeteria or out in the fresh air, they'd immediately be covered in bacteria, and they'd have to put on new clothes. If someone in the OR is just a little bit sloppy, bacteria can enter the room—and within a few minutes there would be more bacteria crawling around than there are letters in this book. Bacteria are so strong that it's almost impossible to get rid of them for any length of time. There are even bacteria that can survive traveling through space on the outside of a spacecraft for more than a year.[7]

A Round of Applause for the Bacteria?

That explains all the attention for these tiny little creatures. They're the simplest life-forms on Earth. They exist closest to the boundary between living and not living. But they're also among the oldest life-forms. They can be found in the deepest oceans and on the highest mountains, the coldest polar regions and the hottest deserts, the most toxic lakes and the deadliest volcanic zones. Just a spoonful of soil contains more bacteria than there are people on Earth. So bacteria are quite remarkable. Most important, without them, the other life on Earth as we know it wouldn't exist.

What's that? A round of applause? For the bacteria? No way! Are you crazy? Who's going to applaud bacteria?

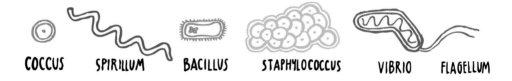

COCCUS   SPIRILLUM   BACILLUS   STAPHYLOCOCCUS   VIBRIO   FLAGELLUM

THE BLACK MONSTER AND DEATH

Bacteria come in all shapes and sizes. There are even luminous ones! Some predatory fish in the sea can't live without them. Take anglerfish, for instance. They're monstrous fish with a spike on their backs that has a bag of luminous bacteria on the end, like a kind of wobbly lantern. It would be useless in bright, shallow water, but these creatures live deep beneath the surface of the water. So deep, in fact, that the sunlight can't get through. It's darker down there than a moonless night in an abandoned coal mine. But you can still see those little lights. The anglerfish happily wave them all around. That's how they attract curious fish. But those fish never get to find out exactly what kind of lamp it is. As soon as they come anywhere near the

anglerfish's gaping jaws, they get sucked down into the creature's stomach at a horrifying speed. Sad? Yes. But that's just life when you're prey (that's what we call animals that get eaten by other animals).

What Could Be Sadder than Dying?

Just imagine what would happen if no fish ever died. Now that really would be sad. A fish can easily lay around a hundred eggs a year,[8] which produce 100 more fish. If those 100 fish have babies of their own, that makes 100 × 100: 10,000. And if they all have little ones, that makes 1 million. Within only three years! And a year later, that's 100 million of them. A year after that, it's 10 billion and another year later, that'd be . . . um . . . loads more. Within 10 years, so many fish would have been born that the entire planet would be covered with a thick layer of fish and fish eggs. And that would really stink.

So, it's good that animals eventually die. Sometimes they die of old age. But fish don't have walkers, false teeth, and retirement homes. Maybe an early death in the jaws of a predator is better than growing old and feeble. If you look at it that way, nature works perfectly: slipper animalcules eat bacteria, small and young fish eat slipper animalcules, predatory fish eat small fish, and so on. The animals keep their numbers under control, and there are never too many of a particular species for too long. It's worked that way for hundreds of millions of years. And if nature worked any differently, you and I would never have existed. It almost makes you want to cry out, "Yay for nature!"

What Works Better than Nature?

All the cleverest brains in the world wouldn't be able to come up with anything that works better than nature. In fact, when humans start interfering with animals and plants, it's chaos. In zoos and aquariums, the staff members have to work their socks off to keep everything healthy and alive: animals have to be fed, plants need to be watered, weeds have to be pulled, and so on and so on. Everything happens naturally in forests, jungles, and oceans, with no need for humans to get involved. And it goes on day after day. In summer, fall, winter, and spring. The workings of nature really are another marvel.

OKAY, THEN, JUST ONE MORE MARVEL

Just one last marvel and then we'll really get started. That one last marvel is . . . all of us. You, me, Joe Schmo from Buffalo, and everyone and everything ever born. But let's talk about you first. Whatever age you are, you actually need to add decades to it. Because there was a minuscule part of you that existed even before your mother was a baby in her crib! You come from one of your mom's eggs. And that cell was in her body a few weeks before she was even born. Around nine months before your birth, one of your dad's sperm cells fertilized that egg cell. From that moment, you were off to a fine start—even though you were nothing more than one single cell.

How Did You Grow?

As a single cell, you were only just beginning. The cell divided.[9] And again. And again. Two cells became four, eight, sixteen, thirty-two, and so on. This went on for days and days. You were a microscopically small ball made of dividing cells. But then, after about 14 days,[10] something else happened.

Something quite remarkable. The cells didn't just keep on doubling—they seemed to be following a plan. Some cells became your heart, others became your brain, and others became your bones. Suddenly you had a front, a back, a top, and a bottom.

After four to five weeks, you were still no bigger than a grain of rice. But you'd reached a new milestone: your very first heartbeat! All being well, that heart should beat at least 2.5 billion times.[11] A week later, tiny little stumps began to emerge, which would develop into arms and legs. Slowly, the rest of you began to grow. When you were 12 weeks old, you looked almost like a real baby.[12] You were far too small to survive outside your mother's womb, though. Your brain, in particular, still needed to grow. At that time, you

were growing around 250,000 new brain cells per minute.[13] By the time you were born, you already had a whole lot of brains, which is why your head was so large in comparison to the rest of your body.

Who Put Nature Together So Perfectly?

After around nine months, it was time: you were born. You were done. Ready. Perfect. That one cell had become a little person. But how did that cell know it needed to split? How did some cells know to become heart, lung, right nostril, or left pinky finger? That really is a marvel, isn't it? And what applies to you also applies to every other living creature. How is it that all animals and plants develop from nothing? Who put nature together so perfectly?

Every group of people in the world has asked this question. And every one came to the same conclusion: it must have been designed and created by a god. The Egyptians, for example, thought everything had been made by the god Ptah.[14] He devised the creatures that would inhabit the Earth, and then he spoke their names. As soon as he did so, those creatures existed. The Mayan people believed all life on Earth was created by the gods Tepeu and Gucumatz.[15] The two gods made all of the animals and plants and thought they had done well. They wanted a little appreciation for their work, so they created humans to praise them and their creation. In the Christian, Jewish, and Islamic faiths, there's one god who created everything, in six days. In those stories too, the humans came last: Adam and Eve. And there are lots and lots of other stories about creation.

Who Can Prove How Life Began?

There were once very few people on Earth who doubted that all living creatures, trees, and plants had been created by a god. But all those tribes and nations, with all their different religions and stories about creation, clearly didn't agree with one another. Their stories were very different indeed. And this is still the case. If you ask people from different religions how life on Earth began, you still get a lot of different answers.

Who's right? No religion can prove its version of creation. People were naturally curious, so scientists began to investigate life on Earth and beyond. And that's what this book is about. How do scientists believe life began? How did they discover all of their knowledge and information? And just as important: Are the scientists able to prove their explanations?

CHAPTER 2

How Old Is the Earth?

CARRY 2, DIVIDE BY 6, MULTIPLY BY 3 . . . SO, GOD MUST HAVE FINISHED BY 6:00

To find out *how* life on Earth began, it's helpful to know *when* it began. How old is the Earth, in fact? How old is the universe? Or are they both the same age? And what evidence do we have?

One of the most famous men ever to have calculated the age of our planet was Archbishop Ussher of Armagh. Just before his death in 1656, Ussher came to the conclusion that God created the Earth on October 23 in the year 4004 BCE ("before common era," or sometimes "before Christ" in books that aren't about science). It was a Sunday.[1]

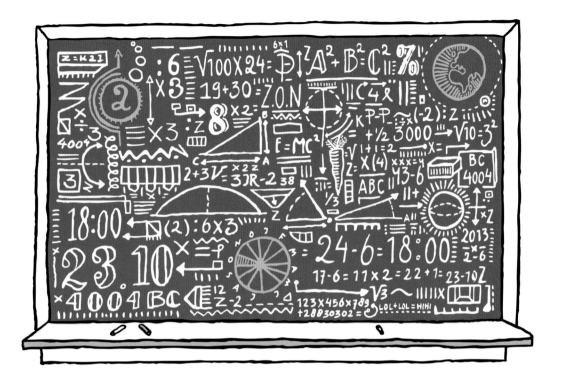

4,000 Years before Common Era—or over 4 Billion?

Ussher was not the only one who attempted to work out the age of our planet. Isaac Newton, for example, one of the greatest scientists ever, used similar methods in a thought experiment to work out how long it would take an Earth-size ball of molten metal to cool: 50,000 years.[2] All of the scientists came up with different results, but they were still fairly similar. That was to be expected, as they'd all used the Bible as their source. Nearly all of Europe was Christian at the time, so most assumed that the Earth must be around 6,000 years old.[3]

There are still many Christians who believe that the Earth is that "young." However, most other religions think the Earth is older. A Chinese folk religion, for example, says that the planet is around 38,000 years old.[4]

And Hindus believe that the Earth and the entire universe are around 4 billion years old.[5] There are a lot more religions with different opinions.

What Are Seashells Doing on Top of a Mountain?

If you go for a walk high up in the mountains, you might spot something you wouldn't expect to find there: seashells. And not just a few, either, but billions of them! It doesn't matter which continent you're on—you can find them everywhere. But how did they get there? Lots of different people came up with the same solution: there must have been a huge flood at some point, a gigantic deluge that made the sea reach the top of the mountains. That explains all of the stories about such an event; the one about Noah's ark is the best known of these tales. But Scottish scientist James Hutton didn't believe the stories. In 1785 he presented another explanation, one that focused on where the mountains, not the shells, had come from.

Hutton noted that mountains can only become smaller. Rocks and boulders always fall down, never up. Sand and stones wash down the mountain, not up. But the Earth hadn't become flatter and flatter—after all these centuries of the Earth's existence, there were still mountains. Those mountains must have grown up somehow. But how?[6]

Hutton could tell from the shape of some stones that they were once molten. He realized that the Earth must have thick liquid inside, like cheese fondue. The hard crust on the outside of the Earth could easily move on the surface of that liquid layer, with some parts of the Earth sinking and others rising. When two parts of the crust collided, mountains could form—just as a wave forms when two flows of water come together, but much, much more slowly. Hutton was unable to confirm his ideas at the time, but scientists nowadays are able to do so. And it turns out that the Scottish scientist was absolutely right: the tops of the Alps and the Himalayas were once seabeds, complete with shells.[7]

You could spend hours, even months, staring at a mountain, but you won't see it move. The speed of mountains moving upward is incredibly slow. Hutton was well aware of that. The fastest-growing mountains rise by only fractions of an inch every year. Transforming a seabed into a mountain that's miles high takes thousands, maybe even millions, of years. Hutton's work told us the Earth must be very old indeed. But how old, exactly?

HOW DO WE KNOW HOW OLD A ROCK IS?

There were already plenty of people studying the stars, animals, plants, and chemical substances, but rocks? Before James Hutton came up with his ideas, this was viewed as a subject that was way too boring to waste time on. Looking at a few pretty minerals or fossils was fun, but studying layers of rock, day after day? That was a different story. Hutton changed all that. He made the science of stones and layers of rock exciting. Geology totally rocked![8]

Geologists made one discovery after another. They came up with a way to classify different layers, so we could tell which time period they were from. They did this with the help of fossils. Wherever you go, you can find in the soil remains of animals that used to live long ago but which are now extinct. And there are more of them than you think. Even though there are so many types of animals and plants now in existence, around 99.9 percent of all species that ever existed have already died out.[9]

How Old Is the Earth, Exactly?

There are plenty of fossils from different time periods. And if two sections of rock contain the same kinds of fossils, they must be around the same age. We also know that the oldest layers are usually deepest in the ground. By

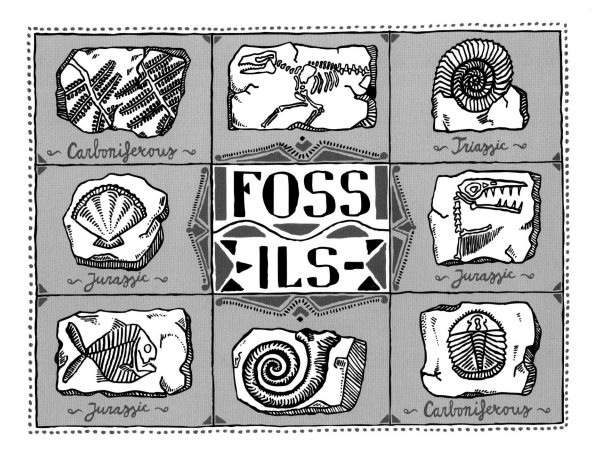

studying the kind of fossils and the kind of rock, it's possible to estimate how old a layer must be.

That's how the geologists used the different layers of Earth to divide up the history of our planet. One of these periods of geologic time is known as the Carboniferous. Layers containing coal were formed during that period. The Devonian is another period; the limestone found in Nevada's Alamo Breccia formation comes from the Devonian.[10] It's a pretty handy way to divide up time. A layer of rock doesn't form overnight, so the scientists knew the Earth must be hundreds of millions of years old. But they still had no answer to that one important question: How old is the Earth really?

Can Rocks Rot and Decay?

It wasn't until 1956 that scientists were able to make a good estimate of the Earth's age. That estimate was still made with the help of rocks and minerals, but also using a very different technique.

Crack an egg, place it under your bed, and wait for a few days. You'll see—and smell!—the effect that time has on certain objects. The egg will rot and decay. That's what ultimately happens to every living thing. But what about things that aren't alive, like rocks?

Rocks don't rot or become moldy. It takes them hundreds of thousands or millions of years to change. But they do change. Like everything in existence, rocks are made up of atoms. And if you wait long enough, every atom changes. Atoms become unstable and lose some of their particles. When that happens, we say that the atom decays. A layer of rock is often made up of various different substances. You can find gold, for instance, or silver, or copper, in layers of rock. These are elements. And the atoms of the different elements decay at different rates. Some of them take a few days, while others take thousands of years.

How Did We Find Proof of the Earth's Age?

Some elements are more unstable than others. Those are radioactive elements, and scientists can use them to calculate exactly how long it takes for half of the atoms in each element to decay. They call this the half-life. To make it difficult, some atoms of the same element have a different half-life time. In iodine, for example, some atoms decay after 52.6 minutes (iodine-134) and others only after 8 days (iodine-131). With some plutonium atoms, it can take up to 24,000 years. Some uranium atoms (uranium-238) can even take 4.46 billion years. So if you find a piece of uranium and half of the uranium-238 atoms have decayed, it'll be somewhere around 4.46 billion years old.[12]

You can see why geology became even more popular after this discovery. Lots of geologists went out looking for the oldest elements.[13] Eventually they found elements that were around 4.6 billion years old. So the Earth must be at least that old. So now we know. Now comes the next big question: how old is the universe? All of the stars, the planets, and the rest.

HOW OLD IS THE UNIVERSE?

How can you work out the age of the universe? Without astronomer Edwin Hubble, we never would have known. In 1929 Hubble made a very important discovery about our universe. He realized that it must consist of untold numbers of galaxies. That was remarkable enough, but he also discovered that all of those galaxies are moving away from one another. Picture the galaxies as small dots on an empty balloon. When you inflate the balloon, the dots move farther and farther apart. The same thing happens with galaxies.

How Can You Work Out How Old the Universe Is?

Imagine making a film of the universe getting bigger and emptier and then playing the film in reverse. What would happen? The galaxies would move closer and closer together. The universe would get smaller and smaller. And smaller. And smaller. Until that absurdly huge number of stars, moons, and planets was compressed into a tiny little dot even smaller than a hundredthousandmillionbillionth of an inch. Is that really what happened? Lots and lots of astronomers think it is.

Most astronomers believe that our vast universe developed from an unimaginably tiny point that exploded, which led to the creation of everything that exists in the universe today. By calculating the speed at which all of those galaxies are flying away from one another, you can work out when this Big Bang took place.[14] Well, that's easy enough to say, but in actuality the scientists still don't have a definite answer. But at the moment they're going for 13.8 billion years old.[15] It's possible that the universe is older, but it won't be much younger than that. And that's to do with the speed of light.

How Long Does It Take a Ray of Sunlight to Travel to Earth?

You'll probably have noticed during a thunderstorm that you see the flash of lightning before you hear the accompanying clap of thunder. That's because light travels faster than sound. Sound travels through air at around

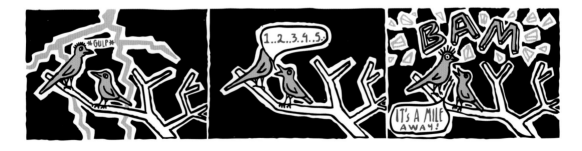

1,125 feet per second, but the speed of light is 186,000 miles per second![16] Inconceivably fast. So fast, in fact, that nothing can travel faster than light. But distances in the universe are also very large. If you're looking through a very strong telescope at someone on the moon who's waving at you, you won't see them until just over a second later. That's because the moon's around 239,000 miles from the Earth. The sun is so far away that its light takes eight minutes to reach our planet. If some bad guy destroyed the sun, we wouldn't know anything about it until eight minutes later.

The other distances in the universe are far bigger. After the sun, the closest star to us is Proxima Centauri. It takes a beam of light about 4.22 years to travel from there to the Earth.[17] That's why scientists prefer to talk in terms of light-years to describe distances within the universe. A light-year is the distance a beam of light travels in a year, which is a huge distance. But even working things out in light-years isn't ideal. There are stars that are so far away from us that their light hasn't even reached us yet. And the most distant galaxy we've ever seen is just over 13 billion light-years away.[18] So the universe must be at least that old.

Now let's go take a look at all the things that have happened in that time.

CHAPTER 3

The History of Everything in 1,620 Words

HOW DID THE UNIVERSE BEGIN?

Have you ever watched a car being crushed into a ball of junk as small as a shoebox? Just imagine a whole apartment block being squeezed into a ball the same size. Now think about our entire planet being squashed until it's the size of a large pumpkin. And, finally, imagine all of the stars, all of the planets, all of the moons, and all of the rocks in the universe being crammed together to make a package that would fit inside the trunk of a car. And then that package being crushed until it's so incredibly small that you couldn't see it with the best microscope in the world, not even if you enlarged it an octillion times. Done it? Now you know what our universe looked like a millionth of a trillionth of a trillionth of a second after the Big Bang.[1]

Now, it is—probably—not true that the universe was very big to start with, and then it was crushed until it was minuscule. I'm just trying to show that the universe and everything in it was once unimaginably tiny. Everything that exists came from practically nothing.

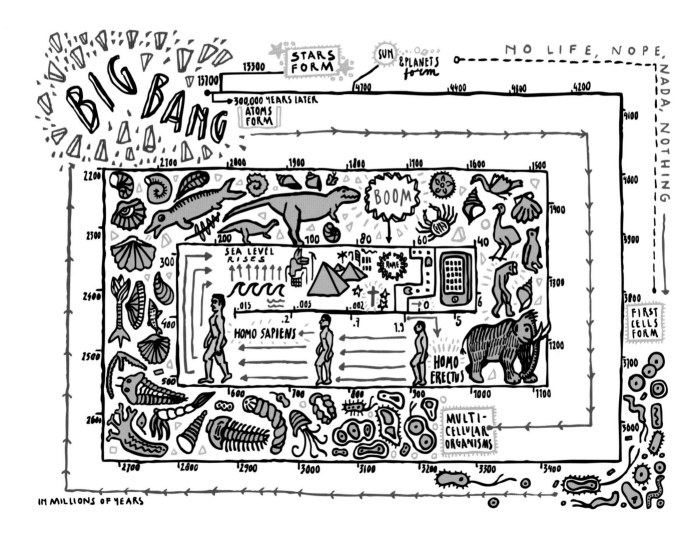

Have Atoms and Molecules Always Existed?

Do you find it hard to imagine all that? That's okay. It really is very hard to imagine that very first beginning, 13.8 billion years ago. But most experts think that's how it happened. The universe was once unbelievably small, and it had a temperature of billions of degrees. Then it burst apart, and it just kept on growing and growing. Within a few trillionths of a second, the universe was as large as a . . . eh . . . very, very large universe.[2]

In that first period of our universe, nothing was as it is now. It was indescribably hot, and there weren't any atoms or molecules yet. The entire universe was still squeezed much too closely together. The first atoms formed 100 seconds after that very first beginning. But they certainly didn't all arrive at once. It was another 300,000 years before all of the atoms existed that make up everything. Our universe had already "cooled down" to around 5,500 degrees Fahrenheit by that point. But there were still no stars or planets. They didn't form until the universe was 400 million years old: 13.4 billion years ago.

How Do You Build a Planet?

When those first stars arrived, they began a dance that's still continuing. Stars form, burn like a candle, and eventually collapse. But that's not the end of the star. A lot of the matter that remains is hugely explosive. When big stars collapse, the particles usually collide so violently that they explode. This happens so quickly and so often that ultimately the whole star explodes. All of the particles shoot into space, where they later cluster together with particles from other stars.[3] Those clusters attract one another and form new stars and planets. But those stars also explode eventually and end up in new stars, and the starry dance starts all over again. Around 4.7 billion years ago, one of these clouds of gas and dust particles was floating through space. Those particles attracted one another. And like water draining from the shower, those particles began to spin and swirl around. This created a flat, rotating disk of gases and lumps. The largest chunk was at the center; it attracted the most gas and dust, and finally it became a star. A few larger lumps of rock and gas went spinning around it. They became planets. That star and those planets are very familiar to us: they are the sun and planets like Mars, Jupiter, and Venus. And, of course, Earth. But Earth then was nothing like the place it is now.

Where Did the Moon Come From?

In the beginning, the Earth was still liquid, but very slowly its outer layer of rock began to solidify. The Earth became a glowing hot ball of liquid rock with a hard crust. Slowly but surely, the Earth seemed to cool and to settle down. Until something came hurtling toward the planet at breakneck speed! What was it? A meteor? A giant space rock? A comet? If only! Nothing less than an actual planet—the size of Mars!—was on a collision course with our Earth.[4] There could be no escape. What happened? An enormous bang that sent chunks the size of countries and cities spinning through space. And while the Earth shook and slowly became a sphere again, those chunks joined together to form a new ball. And that became our moon.

From then on, we had a sun, an Earth, and a moon. Hooray! No, it's too soon for hoorays. Because in the beginning there really wasn't very much happening on Earth. There was no life at all, as it was impossible for anything to live here. If you put together all of the exhaust fumes from cars and all of the gases from chemical plants, sprayed the most toxic substances on Earth into the air, and blew up all of the nuclear power stations and atom bombs on the planet, you still wouldn't come close to making our planet as toxic as it was back then. In those early years, the Earth was still so boiling hot that all of the rock was liquid. But even after our planet had cooled down, it still wasn't a fun place to be.

WHAT WAS A DAY ON EARTH LIKE ALL THOSE YEARS AGO?

What would have happened to you if you were standing on Earth 4 billion years ago? First of all, during the daytime, you'd have burned to a crisp. The Earth had no atmosphere, which is what protects us from the sun today. Sunlight that hits you without that protective layer of air is just as deadly as a nuclear bomb exploding a few miles away. The planet was boiling hot

during the daytime but then cooled down really quickly at night because of that lack of atmosphere. It was completely normal for it to be 0 degrees Fahrenheit in the early morning and 100 degrees by the end of the afternoon. But there was one good thing: the Earth turned much faster than it does now—a day lasted only six hours, or even fewer![6]

It was also impossible to breathe on Earth. There was no oxygen, but instead the Earth was covered with a cocktail of killer gases, such as nitrogen and ammonia. There was also a good chance of a meteorite bopping you on the head. At least 1 million chunks of space rock and ice must have come hurtling from the skies during this period. Fun, huh?

Why Did Life Begin in the Sea?

Those meteorites that battered the planet were what ultimately resulted in the first life on Earth. They brought vast quantities of ice to our planet. That ice melted, creating the first oceans.[7] The lethal rays of sun made life on land impossible, but they couldn't penetrate deep into the water. There were fewer deadly gases in the sea too. Water also warms up and cools down more slowly than land. Once those huge differences in temperature no longer existed, life could develop for the first time. And that's what happened. But it didn't exactly happen quickly.

How Long Did It Take for Life on Earth to Begin?

When we discuss the history of the Earth, we're talking about billions of years, but perhaps it's easier to understand if we switch to millions here. So instead of 4.7 billion years, let's talk about 4,700 million years.

For the first 900 million years (from 4,700 million years ago until 3,800 million years ago) nothing lived on our planet. After that, the first living cells very cautiously conquered the Earth. The following chapters tell you just how that happened. Those cells were the simplest creatures you could ever imagine, but they were most certainly alive. For the next 2,800 million years, not much seemed to happen. The cells did become increasingly complex and sophisticated, though. Just think of the slipper animalcule and the bacterium with its flagellum, which works like an outboard motor. Yet this means that, for its first 3,700 million years, the Earth was inhabited only by single-celled creatures.[8]

And How Long Have Humans Been Around?

About 1,000 million years ago, the Earth was inhabited by creatures that were made up of more than one cell, for example, jellyfish and sponges. But there was still nothing living out of the water. That didn't happen until 475 million years ago. Then the first plants grew on land. Life on Earth suddenly started to develop at a much faster pace: insects appeared 400 million years ago, amphibians arrived 360 million years ago, and reptiles have lived on Earth for 300 million years. Mammals have been here for about 200 million years now. And what about modern humans? We've existed for only 0.2 million years, or 200,000 years.[9]

If you were to cram the history of the Earth into one day, the first living cells wouldn't appear until 4:00 in the morning. Then nothing would happen for ages, until the first creatures made up of multiple cells finally turned up after 8:00 in the evening. At 10:00, the first land animals would arrive. The humans would get there just a few seconds before midnight. And that's the history of planet Earth.

Do You Know Everything Now?

No, far from it. Because you should have loads of questions by now. Like: *Well, how did that first life begin? Where did all the different species keep coming from? Why didn't everything arrive at once?* And, of course: *How do we know all of this?* Don't worry! That's what the rest of the book is all about!

CHAPTER 4

The Greatest Scientific Idea of All Time

WHAT'S THE THEORY OF EVOLUTION, AND WHOSE IDEA WAS IT?

"This is absurd!"

"I've never heard such nonsense."

"How can someone who knows so much be so foolish?"

"The man has absolutely no respect for the Bible!"

= FINCHES =
· VARIETIES[1] ·

CAMARHYNCHUS PARVULUS

CAMARHYNCHUS PSITTACULA

PLATYSPIZA CRASSIROSTRIS

CAMARHYNCHUS PALLIDUS

CERTHIDEA OLIVACEA

GEOSPIZA CONIROSTRIS

GEOSPIZA FULIGINOSA

GEOSPIZA FORTIS

GEOSPIZA MAGNIROSTRIS

GEOSPIZA SCANDENS

SONG FINCH   TREE FINCH   GROUND FINCH

·SEED EATERS   ·CACTUS·FLOWER EATERS   ·INSECT EATERS   ·FRUIT EATERS

"Humans are descended from apes? Ha-ha, is that on the father's side or the mother's side?"

"This notion is not only idiotic, it's scandalous!"

Angry reactions like these were prompted by a book that Englishman Charles Darwin wrote about the origins of all animals, plants, and other life-forms on Earth. The reactions were harsh, but then, Darwin's ideas were also extreme. Darwin was born in 1809. In those days, everyone around him believed that God had created the Earth in six days. But

Darwin came along with a completely different explanation. He wrote that all life-forms on Earth have common ancestors. Humans were not related only to apes but also to azaleas, cucumbers, bluebottles, and bacteria. Darwin claimed that everything that had ever lived, from fruit fly to whale, from cow to cowslip, and from arctic fox to desert rat, came from one single ancestor that had once lived somewhere long ago. It was a bizarre idea, of course. But he was right.

A Doctor Who's Scared of Blood?

Charles Darwin's book completely changed the way biologists and scientists thought. He was always an extraordinary person. As a child, he collected everything he could lay his hands on: shells, animals, coins, stones, and much, much more. He also read dozens of books about animals, plants, and rocks. When he grew up, he studied to become a doctor. However, he soon found out that he couldn't stand the sight of blood, which would obviously be a bit tricky for a doctor. He neglected his medical studies and instead went to lectures about nature. His father didn't approve. He wanted his son to study theology so that

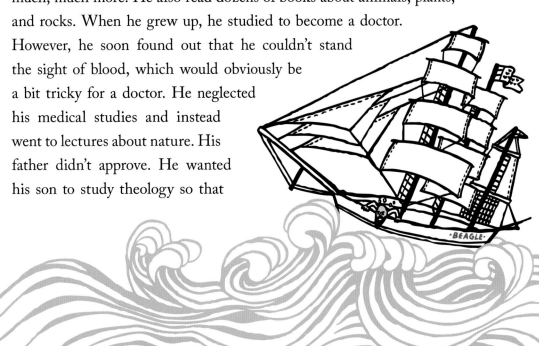

he could become a clergyman. Darwin successfully completed his religious studies. But before he could take up a position as a clergyman, he received an unusual offer: he was invited to go on an ocean voyage around the world as a naturalist.[2]

Where Did All Those Species Come From?

For Darwin, this journey was both heaven and hell. He became seasick very quickly—as soon as the ship left the harbor, he started vomiting over the rail. Whenever they dropped anchor, he would go off to do his research. He was an outstanding researcher. He found a wealth of unusual animals and plants and discovered magnificent fossils of extinct species. What really fascinated him were the differences between certain species. On the Galapagos Islands, for example, he saw different species of birds on each island—all finches, he thought, but all just a little bit different from each other. The birds on one island had beaks that were slightly longer than those on another island. Their behavior was different, too, and they ate different food. And yet the islands were only a few dozen miles apart. Darwin was amazed. He took all kinds of birds back to England with him so that he could study them later. Some of the birds that he had believed to be separate species later turned out to be the same species. But he wondered where all those differences came from. A species of finch on a British island looked exactly like the species of finch in London. Why was it that these birds on the Galapagos Islands were so different from one another?

This question continued to fascinate Darwin. He also became very interested in the methods of animal breeders and plant cultivators. How did they manage to breed and cultivate completely new species and varieties? The answers were simple.

HOW DO YOU MAKE A 200-POUND DOG?

If you want to cultivate tall sunflowers, you use the seeds from the tallest sunflower you can find. Just as children grow up to resemble their parents, plants also resemble the plants they came from. The seeds of a tall flower will produce other tall flowers. To grow tall sunflowers, you plant the seeds of the tallest sunflower you can find, and then you wait for them to grow into sunflowers. Some of those new sunflowers will be even taller than the mother flower. You use those sunflowers to grow even taller sunflowers. And you do the same over and over again, until you finally get sunflowers that are over 10 feet tall. It works the same with dogs. If you want to get big dogs, you need to keep breeding the biggest ones with

each other. That's how we now have dogs in all kinds of different shapes and sizes—from the tiny Chihuahua, which weighs the same as a bag of sugar, to the huge English mastiff, which can easily weigh as much as 200 pounds.

Do You Have the Same Ancestors as an Earwig?

While Darwin was still wondering where all those different species came from, he read a book about population growth—he was interested in lots and lots of different things. It was that book that gave Darwin the new insight that was to make him world famous, the insight that would lead to the greatest scientific idea of all time. The insight that helped to explain why there are so many different life-forms on Earth. And the insight that explains why you, the jellyfish, and the earwig all have the same ancestor. And that insight is: *populations can grow much faster than their food supply.*[3]

Um . . . hello? Is that all? Is that really so spectacular? Yes, it is!

That one little sentence has huge consequences. Just imagine: you're a Darwin's finch (as the birds later became known) on one of the Galapagos Islands. There's only a limited amount of food to be found on such an island. After all, there's not an infinite number of insects, seeds, or berries. In a good year, there's a little more to eat, but just as often there's a little bit less. Whatever the case, the food supply can only increase by a small amount at most. But the number of finches can grow much, much faster. Finches have around 3 babies a year. If each of those baby birds goes on to have 3 babies, you get 9 finches, which is manageable. But a year later, they have 27 more. Those 27 go on to have another 81. They have 243. They have 729. They have 2,187. They have 6,561. They have 19,683. And within a decade, the whole island has become one great big aviary for Darwin's finches. But that's not how it works in reality. Because there can never be enough food for all of those finches.

Which Animals Survive and Which Ones Die?

Not every finch will survive. A huge number of birds die. But which finches will survive? It certainly won't be the weakest and puniest ones. Okay, so which ones will it be? If there are lots of finch-eating hawks around, then finches with better camouflage will be more likely to escape the hawks' claws. If there aren't many hawks but plenty of nuts and seeds, then birds with big strong beaks have the best chance of survival. If there are lots of insects, then the speedy insect catchers are the most successful birds. And here's the point: all of those islands are a little bit different. Slightly different plants grow on one island than another. And you'll find hawks on one island but not on another.

HOW DO YOU MAKE ONE FINCH INTO TWO?

Now imagine that you chased away all of the existing finches from the Galapagos Islands. In their place, you release one kind of finch, the kind you find in woods and gardens back home, for example. What will happen then? Not much at first. The finches are all very similar. They're the same color and have the same beaks and eating habits. And yet there are tiny little differences between them. On an island full of hawks, the finches that are just that little bit closer to the colors of the island will have a slightly higher chance of survival. The same applies to their descendants. Slowly but surely, over generations, the colors of the feathers will move toward being the colors of the surroundings. Within a few dozen years, there will be finches that are a different color than the original ones. The same happens on other islands, too, but the changes affect, say, the birds' beaks or their eating habits. If you wait long enough, there will be more and more differences between the finches. You start with just one species, and you end up with, say, 15 separate finches. Ultimately, the species will be so different that they will be unable to breed with one another to make baby finches.

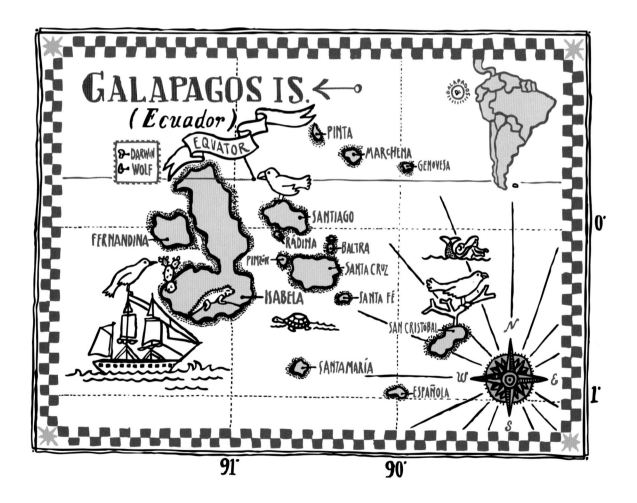

Does All Life on Earth Have Just One Single Ancestor?

The important thing about Darwin's discovery was that animals and plants are able to change over the course of time. Not from one day to the next but certainly over the course of tens, hundreds, thousands, or millions of years. And the animals and plants change, or adapt, as their environments change. Over long periods of time, the Earth changes quite a lot. If, around 250 million years ago, I'd been living in the area that's also my present-day homeland, the Netherlands, I'd have been nice and warm. This part of the world was around the same temperature back then as Spain is now. But if I'd been living here around 140,000 years ago, I'd have wanted to get out as quickly as possible. It was so cold that both summer and winter were freezing. The north of the Netherlands was covered by a layer of ice that was about 1,000 feet thick.

As the Earth changes, the animals and plants that adapt most success-fully have the greatest chance of survival. This is called natural selection. The way that species adapt is by changing, or evolving. That's why Darwin's discovery is known as the theory of evolution. Until now, I've spoken only about finches. But Darwin discovered that there are huge similarities between all kinds of animals and plants. He concluded that all species must once have had a common ancestor. And all of those species had split off from that common ancestor, like the branches of a tree. If you go back far enough, billions of years back in time, you'll come to that one common ancestor.[4]

Why Did It Take Darwin 20 Years to Write His Book?

At first, Darwin's theory was just one of his ideas. He pondered it for years. He knew he wanted to write a book about it one day, and that any such book would turn the scientific world upside down. He also knew it would be viewed very critically—by scientists but also by religious people. Darwin kept on collecting material and reading books in order to come up with as much evidence as possible. He worked on it for 20 years. And he would probably have continued to collect evidence if events hadn't taken a different turn.

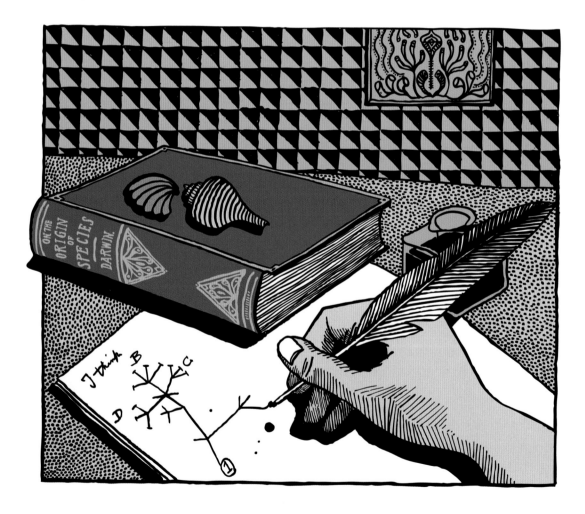

DID EVERYONE THINK DARWIN WAS CRAZY?

In June 1858, Darwin received a letter from a man named Alfred Russel Wallace, who had written an academic paper. The title of his paper was "On the Tendency of Varieties to Depart Indefinitely from the Original Type." It was exactly the same story that Darwin had been working on for 20 years. And Wallace was going to receive all the credit for the idea! It gave Darwin the fright of his life. He wrote a letter back to Wallace and suggested that the two of them should jointly present their ideas about the theory of evolution to a meeting of a scientific society. Wallace thought it was a good plan. But at the last minute Darwin couldn't attend the meeting, and Wallace was far away on the Maluku Islands. So other people had to read out their words. Oddly enough, nothing happened after the lecture. The audience barely reacted at all, in fact. The people who had been at the meeting weren't the slightest bit angry or critical.[5]

Does Everyone Believe Darwin Now?

This calm reaction from the audience was, of course, a relief for Darwin. But he realized that he needed to hurry up with his book. His masterpiece, *On the Origin of Species*, was published a year later. At the start of this chapter, you read some of the kinds of things that people said when it was published. Those were negative comments, but in general the reactions were better than expected. Darwin had backed up his idea with such strong evidence that most readers agreed with him. Not everyone was as angry as those who made the comments you read a few pages back. People made remarks like these:

"Descended from the apes?! My goodness, let's hope that's not true. And if it's true, let's hope that it does not become widely known!"

"People may make their jokes about Darwin's books, but I would rather be descended from an ape than a man who uses his great faculties and influence for the purpose of ridicule."

"A very nice book. But a pity there's not more about pigeons in it. Everyone wants to know more about pigeons. If he had written more extensively about pigeons, the book would sell far better."

Well, maybe those remarks were not really the support Darwin was looking for. But the support came. All the support he could hope for. Darwin's book received a huge amount of attention and sold many copies. His book is now over 150 years old, and people are still reading it. It made Darwin famous all over the world, and he is still regarded as one of the greatest-ever scientific pioneers. For Wallace, it was a different story. He became involved with many controversial ideas, and his reputation suffered. He is still, however, regarded as an important figure who made tremendous contributions to science and other areas.[6]

Are All Species Constantly Improving?

This is not the entire story of evolution. Even now there are still plenty of people who don't believe Darwin. Evolution is an immensely tricky subject. That's why Darwin took so long to gather all of his evidence and arguments. His theory seems logical at first glance, but when you think about it for a while, you realize that it's made up of complex issues that aren't so easy to explain with the theory of evolution alone. For example: the first cells on Earth had no eyes. So where did our eyes come from? How can something as basic as a simple cell eventually develop into, say, a human or an elephant? Does evolution mean that everything keeps improving? Or is that not how it works?

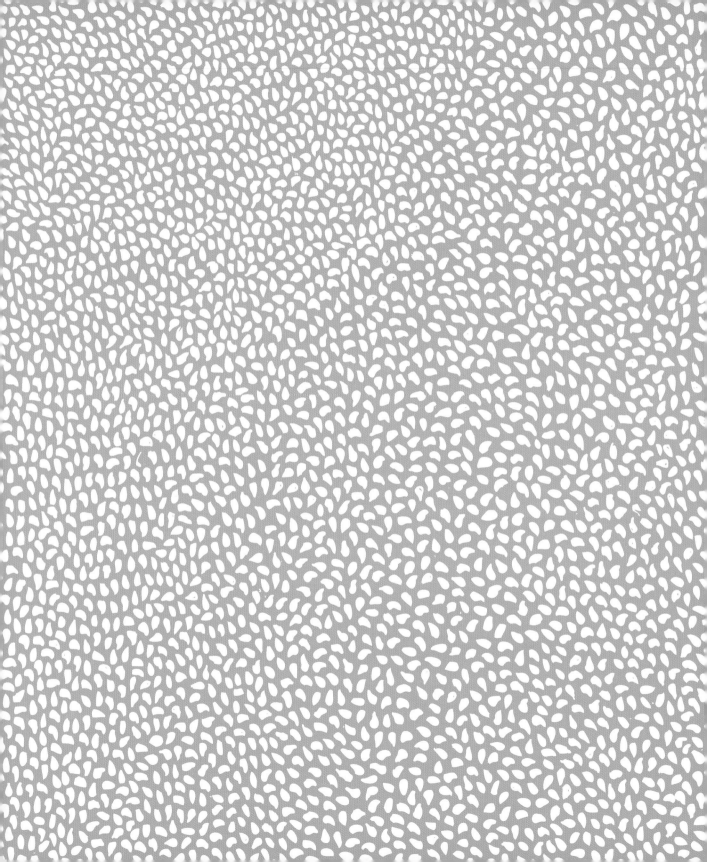

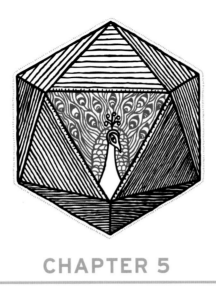

CHAPTER 5

Evolution in Brief

HOW DOES A NEW SPECIES BEGIN?

Darwin's theory of evolution seems simple enough. Take a sheet of blank paper, and do lots of freehand drawings of circles about the size of a quarter. Don't worry if you make any mistakes. Just keep on drawing until the sheet of paper is full. Go on, do it and then start reading again.

Done? You've got a sheet full of circles? Good. Read on!

All of the shapes you drew were circles, weren't they? They all look like one another. But one circle will be a little larger, another not quite so round, and another one might have a small dent. Now imagine if those circles came to life. They'd couple up and have little baby circles. And imagine if there were a predator who particularly liked to eat up the biggest circles. That

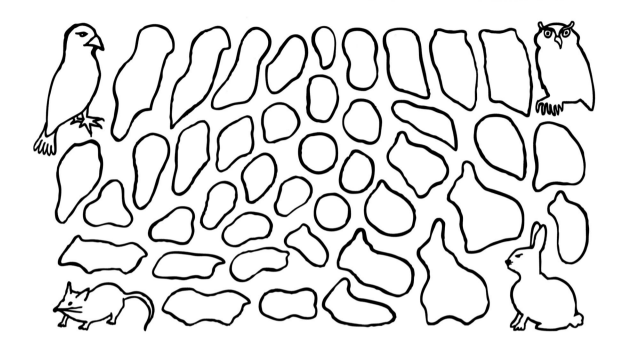

means the smaller circles would have a slightly higher chance of survival. They'd then have babies of their own, and once again, the smaller offspring would have a higher chance of survival. The large offspring, though, would be more likely to die young. Before you knew it, the circles would start to become smaller and smaller. Something similar would happen if the predator started hunting the small circles. As the years went by, the circles would keep getting bigger and bigger. But whatever happened to those circles, eventually a new kind of circle (smaller or bigger) would develop that looked quite different from the original ones. Simple, huh?

It works exactly the same way with animals and plants. Children resemble their parents, but they all look a little bit different. Those small differences may be an advantage or a disadvantage. And it's what the success of their descendants depends on.

Why Do Some Species Change More Quickly than Others?

A living species is never completely finished. If an environment changes, the species that lives there will change as well. And plenty of regions on Earth change. One place might change quickly, while another changes slowly. Temperature and the amount of rainfall have more influence on the Earth's surface than on the sea or deep under the ground. If the temperature or rainfall changes dramatically, that will have consequences for the animals on the land. Those animals will change or maybe even disappear. Because of this, there are species on the land that have only "recently" come into existence, like human beings. And in the sea there are species that have existed for hundreds of millions of years, like jellyfish and worms.[1]

The climate is a major cause of species change. Imagine you're a rabbit, and the climate cools. If snow covers the ground often, your children with the palest fur will be less noticeable to predators. That means they will have a better chance of survival than your children with darker fur. As a result, there will be more rabbits with pale fur. They'll have babies of their own. Again, the baby bunnies with the palest fur will be more likely to survive. So, the rabbits' fur will keep getting a bit lighter over the generations of rabbits. And that process will continue until all of your rabbit descendants are

as white as snow. What happens if the centuries that follow are warmer, and the ground is more often the brown of soil than the white of snow? Then the rabbits will start to become browner again.

Some of the rabbits may have moved south during the cold period, where it was warmer. They didn't need to become white, so they stayed brown. In the meantime, the rabbits who stayed in the cold became white. Eventually you end up with two species of rabbits: white ones and brown ones. And that's the essence of evolution: one species can develop into two or more. When the animals are so different that they can no longer have healthy offspring together, then they've become different species.

The story about the rabbits is just one example. In fact, evolution happens right under our noses. Around 200 years ago, London was an incredibly filthy city, with huge amounts of soot and smoke. This meant that the buildings were very dirty and dark. In those days, there were lots of dark moths around, which were exactly the same color as the bricks. Later, as London grew cleaner, those dark moths became extinct; now the city has paler moths that are the color of cleaner bricks.[2]

It seems that it's sort of possible to predict evolution. With emphasis on the word *seems*, because some pretty strange things happen in nature.

HUH? IT ISN'T ALWAYS THE STRONGEST AND THE BEST WHO SURVIVE?

Lots of people think that evolution's all about the species that is best suited to an environment having the greatest chance of survival. That also seems perfectly logical if you've just read the previous chapter. Why would a species that's best suited to its surroundings not have the greatest chance of survival? Just take a look at great white sharks. Sharks are aquatic killing

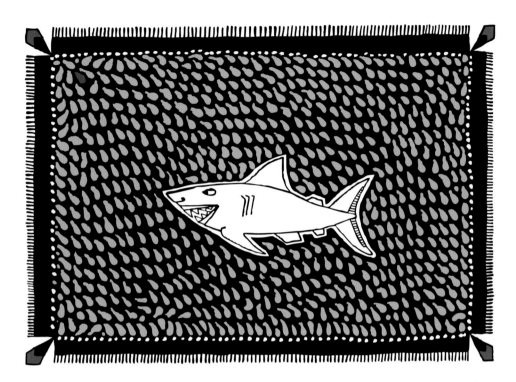

machines: they can smell a drop of blood in millions of gallons of water, easily reach a swimming speed of 25 miles an hour, and take on any prey with their sharp, inward-pointing teeth. If you watch a shark at work, you're seeing the results of hundreds of millions of years of evolution, during which these superkillers have kept on getting faster, stronger, and better.

This is natural selection at work. Sometimes natural selection is thought of as survival of the fittest, the survival of the creatures that are best fit to their environment. However, survival of the fittest doesn't necessarily lead to very "fit" animals. I don't know if you're acquainted with Joe Schmo from Buffalo. But if you know him, then you're aware that he's not the best thing that nature could have produced over billions of years. Joe Schmo has a flabby belly, he can't see a thing without his glasses, and he wouldn't last a week in the jungle. So what's the story with that?

Does a Tree Really Want to Be Tall?

Animals, trees, and plants don't always necessarily become better. They simply change. And that's why they don't always have the most practical shapes. Take trees, for instance. Some trees have incredibly inconvenient shapes. In California, there's a colossal tree called the Stratosphere Giant. It's a coast redwood that's almost 370 feet tall. If it stood beside St. Patrick's Cathedral in New York, it would tower above it quite a ways. But if that giant had been able to choose for itself what it looked like, it wouldn't be nearly as tall. Tall trees catch more wind, and that's no fun. A strong blast of wind could topple them right over. The redwood would probably choose to be shorter, so there's less chance of blowing down. Why is the tree so tall, then? Because trees have always gotten in one another's way. Trees need light. Light provides energy; it's food for the tree. And if you want to soak up light in a forest, you need to grow taller than the other trees. The tallest tree gets the most light. That's why the trees kept growing higher and higher. If the redwoods had all agreed not to grow any taller than 30 feet, then they wouldn't have to worry so much about those gusts of wind.

The Stratosphere Giant hasn't even reached its maximum height. Tree experts have calculated that it could grow almost another 65 feet. Then it would stop. Still quite impressive, huh? But why can't other kinds of trees grow that tall? Trees of that height would have to drink hundreds of gallons of water every day. And when a tree becomes too tall, it can't suck all of that water up to its highest branches. It doesn't take much for the water supply to stop and the branches to start breaking. That's why most trees are much shorter. It's all about balance. Trees have to grow tall enough to get enough light but stay short enough not to break. Redwoods have a special strategy that allows them grow taller than other trees. They found a way to suck up the water in the fog around the treetops. The water doesn't have to be transported from the roots to the tops—the highest branches and needles get their moisture from the air itself.[3]

Joe Schmo from Buffalo is proof that species don't always continue to improve. And he's not the only one. Every plant and every animal has room for improvement. Think about those rabbits again. If, in all the millions of years they've existed, they'd only become "better," they would look different now. Rabbits' eyes are nowhere near as good as the eyes of their enemies: birds of prey. A rabbit with better eyesight has a greater chance of survival than a rabbit with poor eyesight. Why have those eyes not developed more successfully over the past millions of years? It's not to give foxes and wolves a chance. No, there's something else going on.

HAS EVOLUTION MADE A MISTAKE?

There was once a giant species of deer with antlers so large that the males could hardly move. Peacocks have tails that can grow to five feet long.

Bowerbirds fritter away months of their valuable time building a beautiful but pointless work of art. The deer, like the peacocks, lived in an environment with lots of predators. And the last thing you need when you're being stalked by a pack of wolves or a tiger is a set of heavy antlers on your head or a five-foot tail following you around. So why do these creatures look the way they do? Don't bowerbirds have better things to do with their time? Has evolution made a mistake?

Are Females Crazy?

Darwin struggled for a very long time with the problem of evolution being wrong but finally came up with the answer: it's all the fault of the females.

Female bowerbirds don't go for males who build a safe and boring nest. They fall for artists—for the Rembrandts and van Goghs of the bird world, who make the most beautiful and colorful works of art. By the way, what the males build isn't even a nest. They make a bower, a kind of small building or garden house. It can't be used as a nest. Later, when the female wants to lay her eggs, she has to build her own nest.[4] Female peacocks, known as pea-hens, also have strange taste: they go for the males with the most beautiful and longest tails.[5] And female deer fall head over hooves in love with males with enormous antlers on their noggins.[6] If all of these females chose more wisely, animals would be designed a lot more practically, wouldn't they?

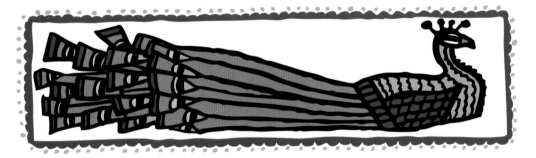

Those females must be crazy! Take the bowerbirds, for instance. There are a number of species of bowerbird, but every male builds his work of art in pretty much the same way. First he chooses a suitable spot for his bower. Then he hops over to the nearby bushes and branches and picks off all of the leaves that might block the sun and stop it from shining on his art. He sweeps the ground completely clean of leaves and weeds and lays a bed of hundreds of twigs. The twigs are woven together so tightly that they're as sturdy as a wooden floor. He inserts other, longer twigs into the base as walls. Again, he uses hundreds of twigs so that the walls are a couple of inches thick. Finally, he makes his work of art even more beautiful by adding all kinds of colorful objects; blue is a particularly popular shade for decorating.

How Does a Bird Make Itself Seem Bigger?

A bower can be decorated with all kinds of things. One bower was found to be decorated with six kinds of berries, two kinds of nuts, three sorts of petals, eggshells, fungi, reptile skin, snail shells, blue and pink stones, aluminum foil, ashes, three different colors of plastic, electrical wiring, insect shells, bones, and manure. And that was just one bower . . .

There are other ingenious tricks to building these works of art. Some bowerbirds place stones in their bowers. They put small stones at the front, where they sit, and bigger stones at the back. Clever! Stones that are close

PTILONORHYNCHIDAE

PTILONORHYNCHIDAE

seem larger than stones in the distance. Putting the smallest stones at the front and sitting on them makes the birds appear larger. They're creating an optical illusion. And they have another neat little trick: an entrance is oriented to catch as much of the sun as possible. That means the males can stay nice and warm—and they're also easier to admire.

WHY DO FEMALES WANT A MURDEROUS IDIOT TO FATHER THEIR CHILDREN?

A male bowerbird spends months, sometimes nearly a year, making his bower. The male must be some kind of idiot to waste all that time on a useless bower. Unfortunately, though, it's his only way to find a lady friend. He has to get down to work. It's also more dangerous than you might think. Some bowerbirds even go so far as to kill other birds and pluck them because their feathers happen to be just the color that the bowerbirds need. They can also seriously wound themselves in the process. Those bowerbirds! They really would do anything for love.

It's clearly not easy to build a bower. The youngest males are no good at it. They learn by watching older birds very closely over the years.[7] That's the point. The females aren't crazy at all. If a female sees a magnificent work of art, she knows she's dealing with an experienced male—a male who's good at surviving and who has enough time to spare to create a beautiful work of art. He's got to be a strong and healthy male, the kind of male you'd want to father your children.

Why Do Peacocks Have Such Long Tails?

With peacocks, it's a slightly different story. Male bowerbirds can easily flee in case of danger, but peacocks are stuck with that unwieldy tail. And yet the

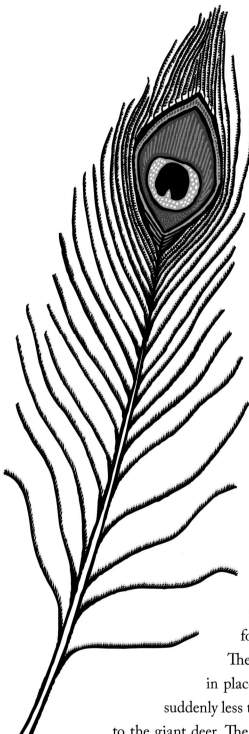

tail is the very thing that attracts the females. If you clip the most popular male's tail feathers, the females suddenly start ignoring him. If you then glue the feathers onto an ugly little male, the females immediately fall for the puny imposter. It's all down to the fake tail. Why? Because unhealthy, weak peacocks can never have beautiful long tails. Sick peacocks have ugly feathers. Healthy ones do not.[8] What's more, they also manage to survive in spite of those huge tails. So a handsome peacock has to be strong, clever, and healthy. A suitable candidate to father little peacocks, in other words. It's exactly the same with other birds. The male robin with the reddest breast is also the fittest. And the birds of paradise with the longest and most colorful feathers are the healthiest. Female birds aren't crazy; in fact, they're plenty smart. At least, most of the time . . .

Why Did the Giant Deer Become Extinct?

What about those giant deer with their supersize antlers? They did become extinct. The giant deer found it easy to survive when there was enough to eat. The same applies to peacocks and bowerbirds. They live in places where it's easy to get hold of food. But if there's suddenly less to eat, they have a big problem. That's what happened to the giant deer. The climate cooled, so they couldn't find as much food.

The deer's antlers became too heavy for deer who needed to travel to find food. Other species of deer with smaller antlers could more easily travel greater distances to get food. And so the giant deer died out.[9] Nature's all about balance, whether it's the height of the trees, the length of the peacocks' tails, or the weight of the deer's antlers.

WHY IS NO ONE PERFECT, EVEN AFTER ALL THOSE MILLIONS OF YEARS OF EVOLUTION?

In nature, it's usually the females who decide on the mate. That's why they play such an important role in evolution. As we saw above, this allows species to develop that aren't always entirely practical. Darwin called this process sexual selection. Along with natural selection, he regarded this as the most important cause for the changes in species. There is constant interaction between these two factors. Sometimes it's useful to look beautiful; sometimes it's better to be fast and strong.

Why Do Women Grow More Beautiful, but Men Don't?

With people, it can be different. Other factors do come into play when humans choose their mates: they might pick someone who's intelligent, or who is wealthy, or who has a great personality. Men often choose the most beautiful women, and women are not always as quick to consider a man's appearance. A more-beautiful woman will find a husband and have children more quickly than a woman who is less beautiful. This results in more beautiful daughters overall in the human species. Men have less need to be as beautiful, and so their male descendants remain just as ugly. What about the sons of beautiful women and the daughters of ugly fathers? They cancel each other out.[11]

Are we smarter than animals for not choosing our partners purely on the basis of their appearance? Not necessarily. Beautiful people often have symmetrical faces. That means the right side of their face is the mirror image of the left. And that's a sign of good health.[12] Men actually may be choosing to have healthy descendants. Smart, huh?

How Do You Become a Super-Rabbit?

Sexual selection and natural selection are the driving forces of evolution. But sometimes they work against each other. And that produces strange

results like peacocks, bowerbirds, and Joe Schmo from Buffalo. When you see a rabbit in a forest, you're not looking at a perfect animal. You're seeing the result of a combination of sexual selection and of adaptations to changes in its living environment. These are big changes, like global warming, interspersed with ice ages and periods of wetness and drought; not to mention volcanic eruptions and meteorite impacts, which have caused huge numbers of animals to become extinct, including predators and competitors; and other changes on Earth, like the emergence of mountains and new islands. And many, many other random events.

If the rabbits' environment changed so that they could no longer live in woodland, then they would have to look very different. They would need to run longer and faster, and they would have better ears. And the little ones wouldn't be born bald and blind but would have a camouflage coat and be able to flee from an early age. Wait a minute! The super-rabbit already exists—it's the hare! You can clearly see that rabbits and hares have the same ancestors. They're very similar, but they're different species, so you can't cross them to make "habbits" or "rares."

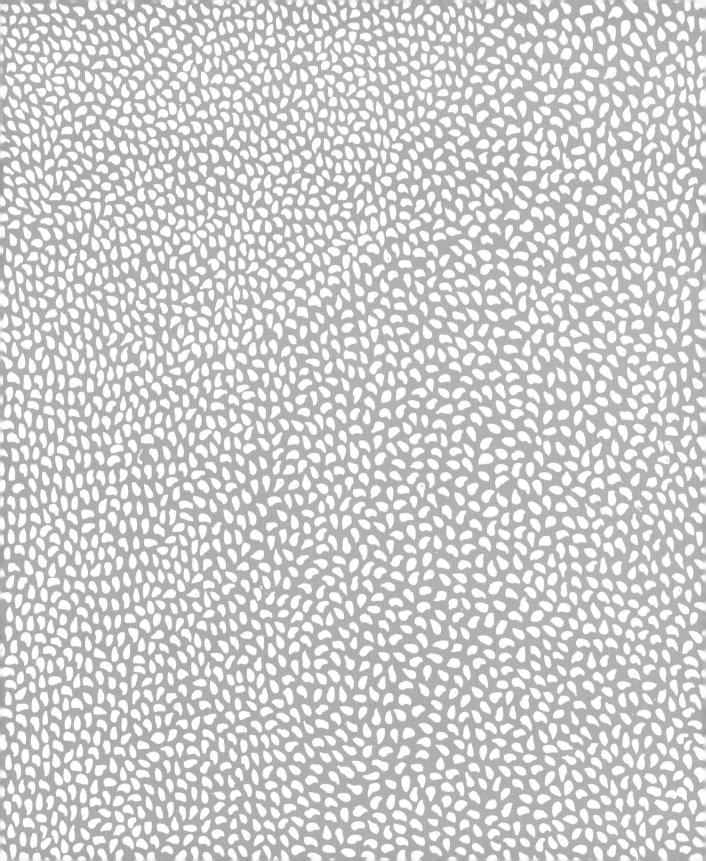

CHAPTER 6

All about the Family

ARE THE MOST SUCCESSFUL ANIMALS TIRED OF LIVING?

Well, we've just about covered everything. We've discussed all of the ingredients involved in evolution, haven't we? Um . . . no. If you look closely at nature, it appears that there are all kinds of exceptions to the idea that it's all about survival in order to create as many descendants as possible. Just take a look at ants, for example.

Of all the species on Earth, ants are among the most successful. You see them everywhere. You can find them in the driest deserts, the wettest swamps, the deepest jungles . . . and in Joe Schmo from Buffalo's kitchen cabinets. If you add all of those ants together, they're heavier than all of the

humans, elephants, and rhinoceroses combined. You can even find some species in the water. Fire ants can make living rafts from their own bodies so that they can cross a river. Or they can make themselves into a bridge so that they can swiftly move their colony from tree to tree. They're intelligent creatures. But not all ants are equally smart.

Did Darwin Get It Wrong?

In an ant nest, there are ants with all kinds of different jobs. There's the queen, who lays the eggs; workers, who take care of Her Majesty, look after the larvae and the little ones, and maintain the nest; soldiers, who protect the nest; and scouts. And it seems that the scouts are pretty dumb. They risk their lives by going out on their own to search for food for the rest of the nest. Without the help of the others, they're defenseless against birds and any other creatures that have *ants* on their grocery list. It makes sense that a smart ant would rather be a queen or a nurse ant instead of a scout. Much safer! But there are always enough candidates who are prepared to take on the dangerous role of scout. Why? Aren't they more likely to die an early death? Hmm.

Another example from the ant world: sick ants don't allow themselves to be pampered by other ants until they eventually recover. They don't get a cozy bed made up for them on the couch, a basket of fruit, or any healing medicines. Instead, they leave the nest. To die! That means they won't infect the other ants in the nest, who will remain healthy. Which is all very nice, of course, but also means that the sick ants have had it. And that is clearly not as Darwin had imagined. Evolution is all about survival and not about dying.

What Animal Would Want to Die?

This strange behavior also occurs in other species. Honey bees, for instance. If you get too close to their nest, they'll soon start stinging you. Bee stings are painful and can cause you a lot of trouble. So you make the wise decision not to disturb the nest. You make a swift escape, with just a few nasty lumps and bumps. But don't go thinking you're the real victim. It's much worse for the bees that stung you; they've lost their sting and now have a wound that will kill them within a day. They've nobly sacrificed themselves for the rest of the nest. Which is very kind of them. But not very smart. Why do they do it? Aren't they supposed to be doing their best to survive?

WHAT ARE GENES, AND WHY ARE THEY SO IMPORTANT?

Why does a bee or an ant sacrifice itself for the group? To answer that question, you first need to know that all of the bees in a hive are related to one another. The same is true of ants in a colony. The workers, soldiers, and scouts are all sisters. The queen's their mother. The babies they look after are their little sisters, with the occasional little brother. Now, imagine you have two nests. That means two "families." In the first family, all the ants just think about themselves, and no one wants to be a scout. The other family, however, does have scouts. The first family will soon die out, because there are no ants to go out looking for new food. Meanwhile, things are going well for the other family. So those ants will stay alive. In short, evolution isn't just about one creature's success and its chance of survival but about the survival of the family. Families whose members have a trait that's good for the whole family, like being unselfish by taking risks to rescue brothers and sisters, will find it easier to survive.

Oh, by the way, in case you are wondering, yes, worker bees and ants do have the potential to become queens and pass on their genes to their descendants. A queen bee or queen ant gives off a chemical that prevents all the non-queen bees and ants from reproducing. When a queen dies, the chemical stops, and a big fight can break out to determine the next queen.[1]

Will Serena Williams's Children Be Good at Tennis?

Not only do ants and bees have a body that has developed through evolution but they also have behavior that's determined by evolution. It's the same for humans. You probably already know that you inherited your funny nose or your bowed legs from your ancestors. But your behavior is also partly the result of evolution. As are your talents. Top athletes often have a sporty mom or dad. A sports-loving parent is, of course, likely to raise a child to love sports, and so there's a higher chance that the child will be good at sports. But upbringing and training aren't enough when it comes to top-level sports. You also need to be born with talent.[2] It's the same for musicians and scientists. But . . . where in your body is that talent located? And who or what decides what you can do and how you behave?

What Do Your Genes Do?

Joe Schmo from Buffalo is a lot like his dad, Joseph Schmo Sr. They have the same physique and also the same posture. They even walk the same. Scientists would say that their physique and the way they walk are "in their genes." Genes are tiny units of molecules within the cells of bodies that function like parts of a code. Every living creature has them, in every cell. The codes in the genes determine the color of your eyes, the way you walk, what kind of beak you have, how long your tail is, what shape your leaves are, what color your husk is, how flexible your trunk is, and where your prickles grow. In short, genes get to decide pretty much everything in every living creature in the world.

The apple doesn't fall far from the tree

Each of the cells in your body contains around 30,000 genes. Those genes determine what the cell has to do. There's a range of genes just for your hair alone, with separate genes for dark or light hair, straight or curly, thick or thin, and so on. And there are genes for the color of your eyes, the length of your nose, and the shape of just about every part of your body. Behavior and talents are in your genes too. There's just one question: Whose talents and behavior do you inherit—your mom's or your dad's?

WHY IS DYING SOMETIMES A GOOD IDEA?

You inherit genes from both your father and your mother. So it's never easy to predict what you'll end up looking like. Will you have your dad's nose or your mom's? Will you have your dad's knack for math, your mom's skill for languages, maybe both, or perhaps neither? It's hard to say. Not every child of a professional tennis player grows up to be a tennis star. But there's more chance of it happening if your mom's a top-seeded player than if she's a concert pianist.

What Could Be More Important than Your Life?

If there are 30,000 genes in a cell, they must be incredibly small. But even though they're so tiny, they're hugely important. Your genes are actually the boss of you. Not only do they determine what you look like, but they also partly decide your behavior. Ants and bees have genes that make them do things that will kill them as individuals but which are good for the genes

THE MYSTERY OF LIFE

72

of the family. That's because the genes of the family members who survive as a result of the noble deed will be passed on. And those genes are almost exactly the same as the genes of the ant that sacrificed itself.

Tricky, huh? It may be easier to understand if you see genes as information for an important mission. Every living creature has its own genes, its own information. But an ant's message is exactly the same as its sisters' message. And that message must be kept alive. The genes are more important than the life of that one ant. And if the ant has to sacrifice her life to make sure the genes are preserved by the family? Then so be it.

You could almost start to hate those genes. There's a good reason why one scientist described genes as "selfish."[3] Genes seem to think only of themselves. Of course, genes don't actually think, because they're not alive. They're pieces of information, and they just happen to have a huge influence on every living creature. And, of course, the scientist knew that very well.

Now you know just about everything you need to know to get started on the most important and exciting part of this book: the part that explains how life first started and how the simplest imaginable cells on Earth ultimately evolved into everything that is alive now.

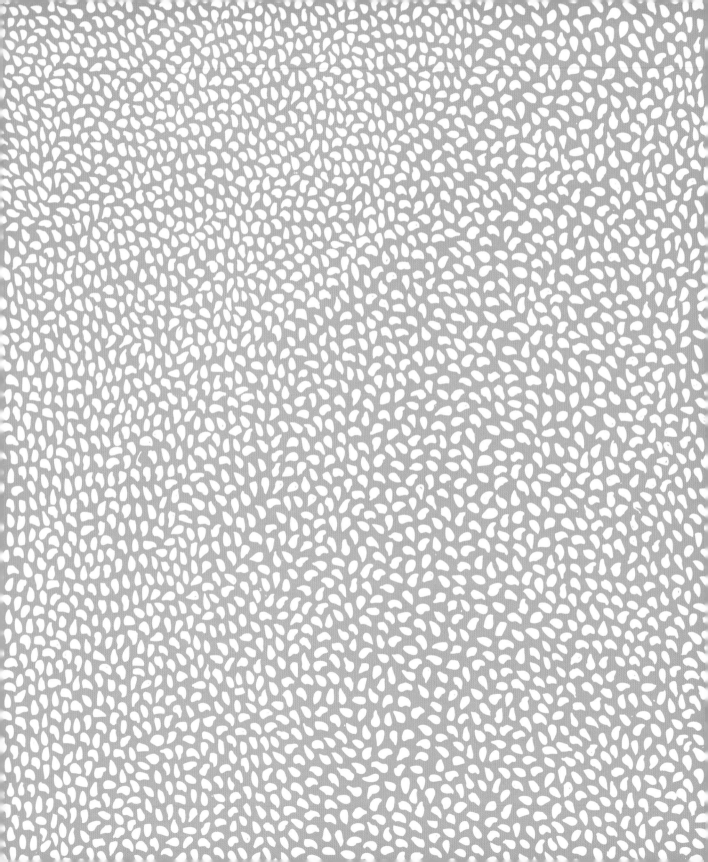

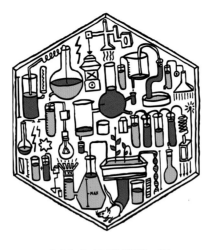

CHAPTER 7

How Life on Earth Began

WHAT'S FRANKENSTEIN'S SECRET?

In the book *Frankenstein*, a young scientist tries to bring dead bodies back to life. He experiments on a few corpses and eventually succeeds in making a monster come to life. It's fun stuff for a book or a horror film, of course. But in real life, it's complete nonsense. We'll never to be able to bring back to life someone who's been dead for days. You'd be better off trying to make a living thing out of a collection of molecules that are as lifeless as a box of Lego bricks. Because that's actually possible. Otherwise you wouldn't be reading this sentence now.

To explain how life came about, we have to go all the way back to the beginning of the Earth. Back then, the Earth was still that boiling-hot

and toxic planet where no known life-form could have lived. And if there was any life at the time, it was wiped out when the Earth collided with another planet. The impact was so violent that nothing could have survived it. Sometime later, life began on this stone-dead planet. For the past few decades, scientists have been racking their brains to figure out how it might have happened. Fortunately, they've already found out a few answers to part of the question.

What Is Life?

Before we can solve the mystery of how life began, we first need to know exactly what life is. Why is Joe Schmo from Buffalo alive, but his watch is not? They both exist. They both move. And if you dropped a 35,000-pound rock on top of them, they'd both stop working. There must be something that makes Joe Schmo alive but not his watch.

Right at the beginning of this book, I talked about dying. Everything that lives also dies. That's what makes the difference between the slipper animalcule and a supermodern robot. It's the same story with Joe Schmo: he can die, but his watch can't. Of course, "being able to die" isn't a useful description of what life is. To qualify as being alive, a living thing has to do a few more things during its lifetime—preferably things that nonliving things can't do.

One thing a watch can't do is reproduce. Joe Schmo can do that. He's the father of his sons, Joe Jr. and Tony, and his daughter, Mo. But reproduction alone is not enough. Because some lifeless things are able to reproduce. Just think about a computer virus—that's a kind of program that can spread via the internet to all kinds of other computers. There have been viruses that started on one computer and infected millions of computers all over the world by the next morning. How's that for reproduction?

Where Did the First Living Creature on Earth Come From?

Something else a watch can't do is eat. Joe Schmo has to wind his old watch every day to keep the hands going around. But there are also watches with

batteries, which makes things a bit less clear-cut. It's almost as if they eat the energy from the batteries. Or what about cars that "guzzle" gas? So eating isn't enough to make the difference. But if something is able to reproduce, eat, and die, then I call this a living thing. At some point in the Earth's history, a living creature developed from a bunch of lifeless molecules. A creature that ate, reproduced, and died. That is, of course, a major marvel. How on earth did that little creature suddenly manage to start living?

WHAT WAS THE SECRET OF THE FIRST LIFE ON EARTH?

The start of life on Earth seems even more incredible when you consider what the world looked like billions of years ago. Not only was the Earth a mixture of toxic substances and high temperatures, but our planet was also blasted by flashes of lightning, deadly sunlight, and countless meteorites. In fact, it was probably that fatal combination that created life, because it's only under these circumstances that amino acids can develop. Amino acids are combinations of molecules that make life possible.[1] Everything that's alive is made of them. They're the building blocks of all cells, animals, and plants. Muscles, for example, can't work without amino acids. That's why bodybuilders stuff themselves with amino acids, in the hope that they'll get bigger muscles just by eating.

How Do You Make Life in a Test Tube?

An amino acid isn't alive itself, but it comes pretty close. Amino acids are as far from living creatures as clay is from a teacup. You first have to mold wet clay into a teacup shape, and then you fire the clay. Only then does the cup become a cup. It works the same way with amino acids. Amino acids have to be transformed into proteins. And proteins are found only in living things. We need proteins to form cells.[2] Our bodies consist mainly of proteins; plants contain proteins; bacteria are made of proteins. In short, proteins are in everything. Proteins, proteins everywhere!

Fine, that's enough about proteins, for now. Time to get back to the amino acids. Where did they come from? Professor Stanley Miller wondered the same thing.[3] And to find out the answer to that question, in 1952 he re-created the Earth, as it was billions of years ago, inside a test

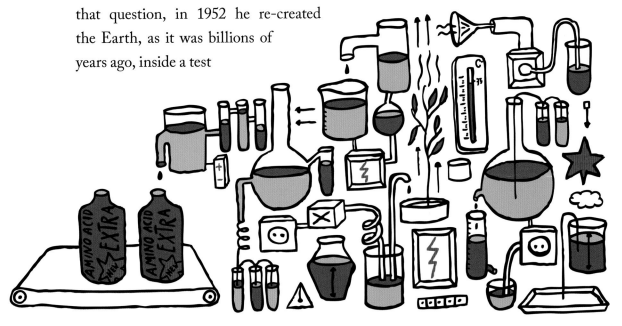

tube. He mixed substances that were around on Earth back then (water, methane, ammonia, and hydrogen gases), heated it all up, and bombarded it with electric shocks in order to mimic the lightning. And what happened? Amino acids formed! Party!

What Is DNA, and Why Does Everyone Keep Talking about It on Cop Shows?

Unfortunately, the professor's celebration was premature. In more recent years, other scientists have discovered that the Earth was not like the version Stanley Miller re-created in his test tube.[4] And yet Miller's experiment was invaluable, as it proved that, given the right conditions, amino acids can form spontaneously.

So we come to the next question: How do proteins form? It's very simple: with the help of deoxyribonucleic acid. Deoxyribonucleic acid is a molecule that converts amino acids into proteins, just as your hand can turn clay into a teacup. Deoxyribo . . . Are you already tired of that word? So were the scientists. And that's why they shortened it to DNA, which probably sounds more familiar. The people who make cops shows on television are crazy about DNA. If you read on, you'll see why. You may well have seen the shape of a DNA molecule before too. It's like a kind of rope ladder that twists around in a spiral. In science, they don't call the shape a twisty spiral, though, but a *double helix*. But anyway, DNA is essential for our life on Earth today.

HOW DO YOU MAKE A JOE SCHMO FROM BUFFALO?

All of the information about what you look like and how you're put together is recorded in your DNA. Some people compare DNA to a cookbook with

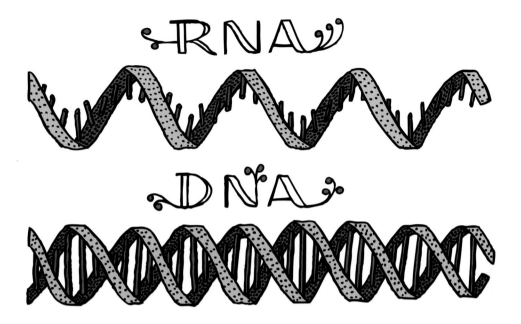

the recipe for a human, animal, or plant. Others see it as the instructions from a construction kit. Every one of Joe Schmo from Buffalo's DNA molecules contains the instructions for how to build a Joe Schmo from Buffalo. But DNA is more than that. You could also see it as a factory that converts amino acids into the proteins that make up all of the parts of your body.

DNA molecules, if you stretch them out, are long strands. Genes are sections of each DNA molecule strand. You could compare a DNA molecule to a very long train. Genes are the train cars. Individuals are different from one another because everyone has unique DNA with unique genes (except identical twins, who have the same DNA and genes). Now you can see why DNA is every homicide detective's favorite three-letter acronym. Every cell in a body contains the same DNA as every other cell in that same body. If a detective has one of the murderer's hairs, he or she can take a look at the DNA inside it and compare it with a suspect's DNA. Are they a match? Then the suspect is the murderer.

Which Came First: The Chicken or the Egg?

DNA molecules are in every living cell, and that means they're very, very small. But the strand of just one of these molecules is over six feet long when you stretch it out! And there are so many cells in your body! If you laid out all of your DNA molecules in one long line, you get over a billion miles of DNA.[5]

Now you know enough about DNA molecules and amino acids to understand the beginning of life on Earth. It's very simple. Billions of years ago, there must have been amino acids, and DNA molecules must also have developed that were able to turn the amino acids into proteins. And therefore . . . um . . . hmm . . . errr . . . Unfortunately, it's not that simple at all. Because DNA doesn't just appear by itself. It needs certain other molecules in order to form. And I'll give you one guess which molecules it needs. Exactly! Protein molecules. You need DNA to make protein—and protein to make DNA. So it's a real chicken-and-egg situation. Which came first: the chicken or the egg? Well, a chicken comes from an egg. And that egg comes from a . . . chicken. The mystery of how DNA first formed is the oldest chicken-and-egg problem on Earth. Life without proteins is impossible. And proteins without DNA are impossible. So life without DNA is impossible. Aaargh!

Has the Chicken-and-Egg Problem Been Solved?

How do you solve the problem of the chicken and the egg? It seems unsolvable. And yet we know there must be a solution, because both the chicken and the egg exist. So there has to be a solution for the DNA-and-protein problem too. The most obvious solution is: RNA. RNA (that stands for *ribonucleic acid*) is a lot like DNA, but it doesn't have that twisty rope-laddery spiral shape. Um, I mean, it's not a double helix. Like DNA, RNA contains information about life. More important, it can copy itself. So RNA molecules were the first molecules on Earth that were able to produce "offspring." Because RNA doesn't require any protein to exist. When life began, RNA might have played the part of proteins and DNA. Later, DNA evolved from RNA, and that produced proteins. There's no definitive proof of all that yet, but scientists are well on their way to finding the evidence.[6]

But that leaves us with another problem: where did RNA come from? RNA is also a long molecule, with a very complex structure. Creating RNA is a bit like tipping a billion cans of alphabet soup into the ocean and waiting for Lady Gaga's lyrics to come washing up onto the shore. It's not absolutely impossible that something like that might happen, but the chances are so small that it's mind-bogglingly unlikely.

WOULD YOU LIKE TO BRING A SUBSTANCE TO "LIFE" YOURSELF?

Fortunately, you don't have to buy billions of cans of alphabet soup to check if RNA can form by itself. RNA is made up of various chemical substances, which have to follow certain laws of chemistry. Some molecules in those substances attract one another, while others repel one another. Compare it to the idea that some letters often appear together and other letters never occur next to each other. In English, you won't come across combinations

① BOIL SOME WATER & POUR IT INTO A CLEAN, EMPTY JAM JAR → HALFWAY

② x3 ADD 3 SPOONS OF SALT TO THE WATER & STIR UNTIL IT DISSOLVES. SALT TIP → ADD A LITTLE DYE

③ TIE a piece of STRING AROUND THE MIDDLE OF A PENCIL →

④ ← CUT HERE PLACE THE PENCIL ACROSS THE TOP OF THE JAR AND LET THE STRING HANG DOWN INTO THE WATER THE STRING SHOULD BE ABOUT THREE INCHES LONG THE STRING MUST NOT TOUCH THE SIDES OR THE BOTTOM OF THE JAR! PLACE THE JAR IN A DRY PLACE WHERE NO ONE GOES

⑤ ~ BUT GO TAKE A LOOK EVERY OTHER DAY... LEAVE IT until all OF THE WATER HAS EVAPORATED → & NO VIBRATIONS! ← X • NO WASHING MACHINES • NO STOMPING • NO DANCING • NO YELLING like *FSDG*, *HHRTRGDD*, or *YYTTYIII*, for instance, but *OHAB*, *YBABA*, and *ABBY* are a lot more likely. From there, it's just a small step to *YEAH, BABY*, isn't it?

You can do a simple little experiment at home to see how it works. Molecules in ordinary, everyday substances suddenly join together to make a string and appear to come to life.

Is Salt Alive?

What happens? A little salt-crystal tree starts to grow. As the water evaporates, the salt crystal slowly creeps upward as if it's a living creature. In reality, nothing in this experiment is alive; the salt's just following the laws of chemistry. The same kind of thing happens as RNA forms, but it's millions of times more complicated. That's hardly surprising, as RNA had hundreds of millions of years to develop. Scientists have carried out their own experiments to make RNA. And they were successful![8] But RNA is less complicated than DNA. So it's almost certain that DNA developed from RNA.

WHAT DID THE EARLIEST LIFE-FORMS LOOK LIKE?

The most basic life-forms that we know on Earth today are very simple cells, like the slipper animalcule. And yet even such a simple cell is still pretty complicated. It's like a small body. It has a nucleus, with DNA molecules and genes. That's a bit like the cell's brain. It has parts with interesting names like ribosomes and mitochondria, which you could call the organs of the cell. It has cytoplasm, which, at a stretch, you could compare to blood. And it has a membrane, a kind of skin that holds everything together. There are quite a few essential elements to keep the cell working. In short, it's a pretty complex thing. That's why it's inconceivable that the very earliest life looked like that.

Those first cells must have been much simpler, not like a little bag with everything all packed up neatly inside. The first cells didn't have a nucleus, mitochondria, and ribosomes. All of those amino acids, proteins, and RNA and DNA molecules were lumped in together. The RNA and DNA molecules gave the instructions to the amino acids and proteins. Together, they did what a cell does: absorb useful substances and get rid of superfluous substances. And cultivate new cells.

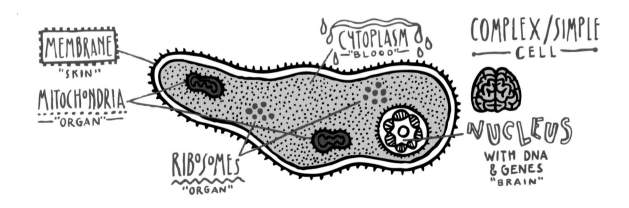

WHERE CAN YOU SEE CREATURES THAT ARE OLDER THAN DINOSAURS?

But how did actual cells form from this stuff? At the beginning there were just RNA molecules and other important chemicals, surrounded by fatty acids. These fatty acids surrounded the RNA molecules, closed up, and became membranes. These became the first protocells, the predecessors of the modern cells. Eventually, all of the elements inside the protocells developed into properly functioning ribosomes, mitochondria, and the rest.[9]

There are still some very simple cells in existence that resemble those earliest closed cells. Certain bacteria, for example. Not those complicated

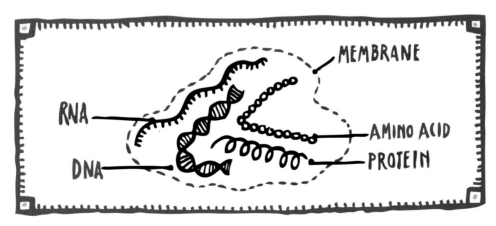

bacteria with a superdeluxe outboard flagellum, though, because it took billions of years of evolution before they appeared. No, I'm talking about very simple cells without a nucleus and mitochondria. Those cells still work so well that they've hardly changed in all those billions of years of evolution. And you can find them everywhere. If you want to take a look at life as it was a few billion years ago, all you have to do is pick up a good microscope, and you'll see creatures that are billions of years older than *Tyrannosaurus rex*! They are called archaea, and we will take a closer look at them later. But yes, unfortunately, they're not quite as spectacular as *T. rex*.

Does the Earth Have a Weight Problem?

There are still plenty of questions about the beginnings of life of Earth. But we're getting a clearer picture of how it might have happened. And I still haven't mentioned the most likely explanation. It has to do with meteorites.

Look out! Duck! As you're reading these words, the Earth is being bombarded with material from space. Meteorites, and also space dust. Every day all that stuff makes the Earth about 200,000 pounds heavier.[10] But don't worry: your chances of being hit are minuscule. And besides, the Earth's so heavy that no one really notices all that extra weight. How heavy is the Earth? Very heavy: as much as 13,170,000,000,000,000,000,000,000 pounds![11] Anyway, some of those thousands of pounds of meteorites contain amino acids. And we know for certain that those substances come from space because sometimes they're completely different amino acids than the ones we have on Earth.

Did Life on Earth Actually Start on Earth?

The universe is, of course, much older than the Earth. And so there's a pretty big chance that amino acids actually arrived on our planet on a meteorite.

Perhaps from a planet where amino acids or their predecessors had already developed billion years of years before Earth was formed. That planet could have burst apart, or perhaps an asteroid impact kicked up some debris into space. And maybe one or more of those pieces of debris with their amino-acid building blocks might have provided the basis for life on Earth.[12]

So, life on Earth could have started in a variety of ways, on Earth itself, or perhaps somewhere else in the universe. This makes it trickier to find definitive proof of the origins of life. On the other hand, all of these different explanations make the beginnings of life seem less extraordinary and a whole lot more logical.

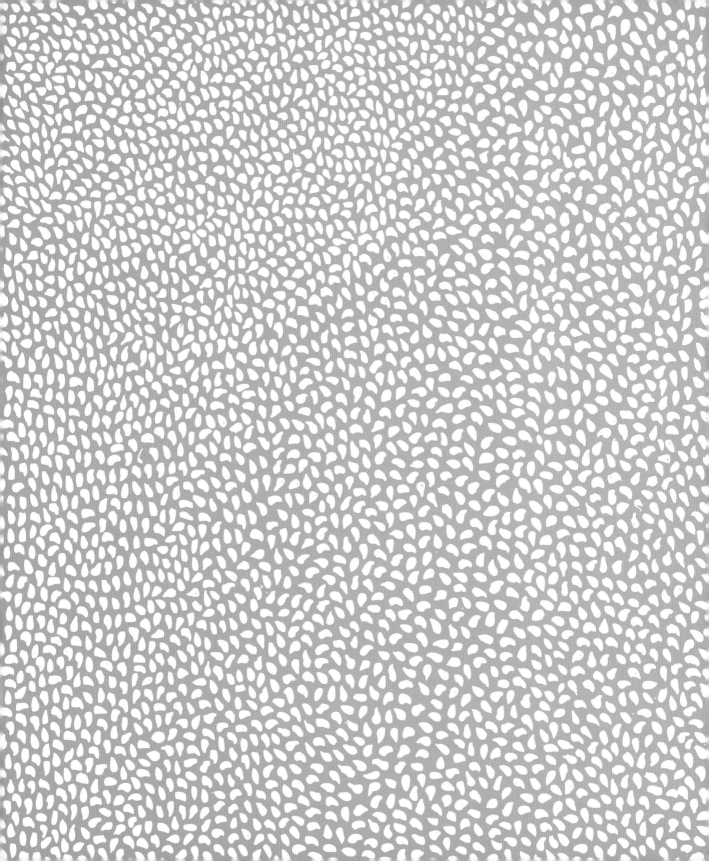

CHAPTER 8

Surviving in the Primeval Oceans

WHERE DID LIFE ON EARTH BEGIN?

Okay, we still don't know for certain how life on Earth began. We don't know exactly *where* it began either. It could have happened in more than one location. One thing is for sure, though: wherever it was, it was in a place that would have been extremely unpleasant for human beings. Because that place had to meet a number of tricky requirements.

According to some scientists, it would have to be really hot—about 160 to 180 degrees Fahrenheit. Below that temperature, not enough happens to the molecules to form amino acids, but above that the molecules can break

apart. But the place can't have been located in the bright sunlight. There was no protective atmosphere around the Earth back then, so every ray of sunlight was fatal. And there must have been water.[1] Life began in a sort of primordial soup, and every cook knows you need water to make soup. If you consider all of the requirements that the place had to meet, then only a few possibilities remain. Let's take a closer look at what those possibilities might have been.

Did Life Begin in Boiling Mud Pools?

Are you on the beach? Do you have a shovel and some time on your hands? Why not dig a hole in the sand, about 4,000 miles deep? You'll end up right at the center of the Earth. It won't be very pleasant there, because it's over 10,000 degrees.[2] The deeper you dig, the hotter it gets. The crust of the Earth is so thick in most places that we don't notice the heat. But there are some spots on Earth where the crust is very thin: Iceland, for instance, and Yellowstone National Park.[3] The crust's so thin in some spots that the groundwater boils and comes spurting out of the ground. That's how geysers are formed.

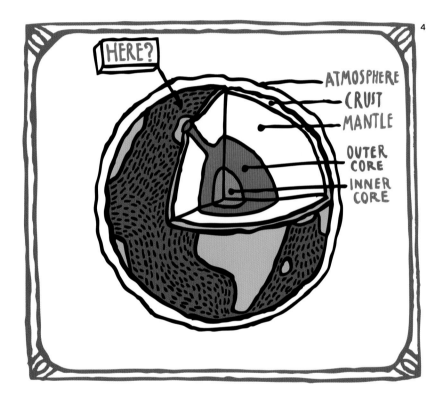

What Can Live in One of the Most Deadly Environments on Earth?

Some lakes and ponds are also warmed by the Earth's heat. Sometimes they're nice little pools where you can take a dip in the winter. But they're just as likely to be stinking, muddy lakes that are so acidic that everything there shrivels, so hot that you could boil an egg in them, and so toxic that just breathing in the fumes can knock you out. That makes them perfect locations for the origin of life!

Hmmm, you're thinking, is it even possible for anything to live there? You bet. There are microbes (that's a collective name for creatures that are too small to see with the naked eye) that thrive at a temperature of over 185 degrees and a level of acidity that could dissolve a bicycle.[5] That's what I call tough!

A boiling-hot mud pool fulfills two of the three requirements for life: it's warm, and there's water. The sun can penetrate the shallow water, but that's not necessarily a problem. These kinds of pools always occur close to volcanoes. And we know that volcanoes were exploding away like crazy back before life began. They must have produced a whole heap of smoke and ash. That could easily have blocked out the bright sunlight. And there you go: all three requirements have been met!

What Are the Toughest Creatures on Earth?

Scientists have fished out various kinds of bacteria from these mud pools, which could be among the oldest species on Earth. They've even found a completely new life-form: the archaeon. And if you're looking for a tough guy, you've come to the right place! Archaea live in the hottest springs; some can even survive a temperature of over the boiling point of water (212 degrees Fahrenheit).[6] Other archaea live in the extreme cold, while others live in environments that are very salty, acidic, or just plain toxic.

Archaea are a lot like bacteria: They're also single celled and just as tiny. And some archaea even have a flagellum, though their flagellum works in a completely different way. But archaea have an entirely different structure from bacteria. Evolution can achieve similar results in different ways. Later on in this book you'll see some even more spectacular examples.

But yes, those hot pools could quite easily have been the source of all life on Earth.

Or Was It the Ocean Floor Where Life Began?

Water, high temperatures, and no sunlight—these conditions are also found at the bottom of oceans. Not everywhere, but in spots where the Earth's crust is very thin. In a few places, the crust is so thin that molten lava seeps out through deep-sea volcanic vents. The water in such places is astoundingly hot; it can get up to several hundred degrees Fahrenheit. Boiling water usually evaporates immediately, but the pressure of the ocean stops the water from boiling. This pressure is so huge that being in it would feel like carrying a mile-high tower of buckets filled to the brim with water on top of your head.

But nothing can possibly live there, could it? No one can survive such pressure, could they? Oh yes, they can. All sorts of creatures live way down at the bottom of the sea, as

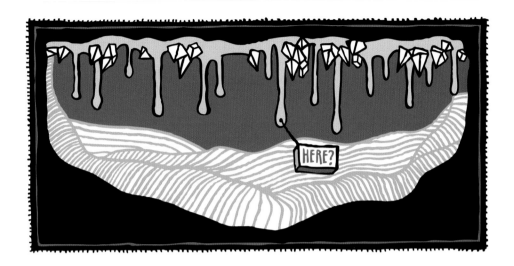

if it were a perfectly natural place to live . . . which, of course, it is. It's home not just to archaea and bacteria but also to worms and snails and shrimps.

Perhaps life really did begin at the bottom of the sea.

Or Could Life Have Started Deep under the Ground?

There's groundwater deep beneath the Earth's surface. There's no sun, but it's warm enough. But is there any life down there? Yes, there is. And it's actually in places that are a lot more inhospitable than seabeds or boiling pools.

Some of the most remarkable life-forms beneath the Earth's surface are called snottites. No, I didn't just make that up. That's what they're really called. They're slimy, gooey bacteria that drip down in caves just like . . . um . . . snot. They live in a deadly atmosphere and feed on toxic substances, leaving sulfuric acid as a waste product.[7] That's an acid that murderers use to dissolve the bodies of their victims so that no one will ever discover even a trace of them.

CAN BACTERIA SURVIVE ON MARS?

But that's nothing compared to some other bacteria! Some of them, like *Desulfovibrio vulgaris*, live in a space without oxygen, without food, and packed with toxic gases.[8] But they're world champions at survival; they've been there for millions of years. What's the secret of their success? Very occasionally they'll munch on a molecule of sulfur or iron.

There are even bacteria that survive under Mars-like conditions. Scientists found microbes that live upon the upper flanks of the Socompa Volcano, high in the Andes mountains. This volcano isn't exactly your ideal holiday hotspot. There's almost no oxygen and a lot of ultraviolet radiation. Where the steam from the volcano bursts through the ground, there's methane and water. Combined with the atmospheric carbon dioxide, the conditions on the volcano resemble what life would be like on Mars.[9]

After all of this, I don't think I have to tell you (but I will): microbes are really, really tough. That means there are at least three possible places where life on Earth could have started.

LET THERE BE LIFE!

And there was life! From that point on, things moved quickly for the descendants of those hot-water-loving cells. Those babies conquered the entire world. There was no stopping them. Some single-celled organisms stayed where they were. Others adapted over the course of millions of years so that they could withstand less extreme temperatures. And others found themselves out in the cold. But all over the planet, wherever you went, the oceans were teeming with single-celled life. What happened next?

Nothing. That's what happened next.

And after that . . . Nope, still nothing.

And then, for millions of years, ab-so-lute-ly nothing happened. Nothing at all.

Yes, of course, the single-celled organisms went on reproducing and all sorts of new species came into being. But you have to admit that it's not very spectacular. For hundreds of millions of years, the Earth was the domain of microbes that did nothing but float around, eat, and reproduce.[10] And then the same again, for a few more hundreds of millions of years.

Cow Pies That Are Millions of Years Old?

This enormous period of time gave single-celled organisms the chance to develop a more complex appearance. Slowly but surely, they grew tiny little hairs, which would eventually lead to that sophisticated flagellum. And a very different kind of creature evolved, a creature that took its energy and food not only from the substances in its surroundings but also from the sunlight. The sun, which for millions of years was more of a destructive force, was now a source of life for some cells.

Traces of the Earth's very first sun worshipers can still be found. Just travel to Lester Park in Saratoga, New York, for example. Or Waterton Lakes National Park in Canada. They're called stromatolites, and

they look a bit like fossilized fungi or overgrown cow pies.[11] They're collections of millions of single-celled organisms, all piled up in a heap. The cells joined together to form a kind of living cow pie. The old dead cells hardened and new layers of cells formed on the exterior. This allowed them to grow into sizable chunks—big enough to be found as fossils 3 billion years later. And . . . as living creatures! Because stromatolites aren't actually extinct. You can still find living stromatolites in a few places on Earth. The most impressive ones can be seen at Shark Bay in Australia.

Who Were the Biggest Polluters on Earth?

As well as the stromatolites, there were other species that took their energy from sunlight. The sun shines every day, so it's an extremely handy way to survive. Most life-forms we know today, such as trees, plants, algae, and seaweeds, live on energy from the sun. And all of them are descended from those very first single-celled sunbathers.

Solar energy gave these new species a big advantage. They quickly spread across the globe. So quickly, in fact, that it caused a huge problem: the new species gave off a dangerous gas that poisoned the planet. They were the first environmental polluters on Earth. And it wasn't just a tiny little bit of pollution either. The gas emissions were so bad that they destroyed nearly all life on the planet. And that deadly, destructive, toxic gas was . . . ? Oxygen! Exactly the same oxygen that just about all life on Earth today depends on. But what doesn't kill you makes you stronger.[12]

HOW DOES A BACTERIUM BECOME A WHALE?

But not all life at the time was wiped out by the oxygen. Such large-scale destruction is no easy task, not even with the strongest of poisons. Farmers who use poisons to protect their crops from pests know that any pesticide works only for a while. At first it will kill almost all of the pests, but there are always a few that survive. They go on to make new pests with the same poison-resistant genes. These creatures will survive and even thrive—until the poison no longer kills any of the pests. That's what happened with oxygen all those millions of years ago. Bacteria and archaea came along that learned to live with it. And all of the fish, reptiles, birds, and mammals on Earth are descended from those single-celled organisms. From begonias to bunnies, bonobos and blue whales: they all share that microscopic ancestor.[13]

Something as small as a bacterium needs a very important characteristic in order to evolve into something as large as a whale: it has to be able to cooperate. Think about it: all cells are tiny. There are no giant cells. You can just about see the largest cells with the naked eye. You won't find any bigger cells anywhere. If something really wants to expand, it has to be made up of multiple cells. For the first hundreds of millions of years of evolution, that was impossible. But the new substance, oxygen, suddenly created all kinds of new opportunities.

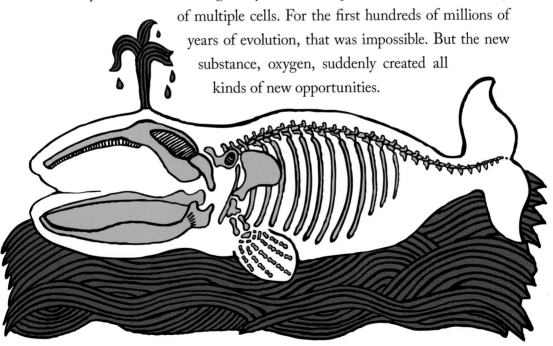

THE RESURRECTION OF A SPONGE

1 HOUR ⟶ A FEW WEEKS

What Happens When You Put a Sponge in a Meat Grinder?

The oxygen allowed completely new proteins to develop, which meant that many kinds of new cells were able to form. Some of those cells contained the substance collagen, a kind of glue. The cells could stick together, and so were able to grow into larger collections of cells. That's how we got trees, whales, fungi, and, of course, Joe Schmo from Buffalo. You can see just how handy collagen is. That's why it's one of the most abundant proteins in the animal world.[14]

Sponges are a good example of creatures composed of multiple cells. They're among the oldest multicellular organisms in existence. With sponges, you can clearly see how the move from one cell to many worked. Because sponges have only a few kinds of cells. They have no nose, heart, or brain—and they certainly don't have eyes or square pants! (There is, however, a fungus called *Spongiforma squarepantsii*, which was named after SpongeBob SquarePants). Most sponge cells have the same function. You'll discover that for yourself if you do an experiment with a live sponge. You can cut a sponge into pieces and put it through a meat grinder. Then you can press your minced sponge through a sieve. And you can whisk up the minced sponge with a mixer. If you put the resulting mixture into a container of water and wait for a few weeks, a completely new sponge will form. All of the cells clump together again as if nothing had ever happened.[15]

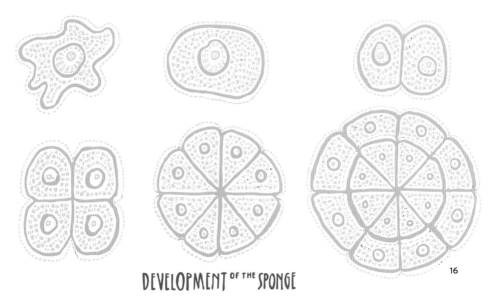

DEVELOPMENT OF THE SPONGE [16]

HOW DO YOU MAKE A PLASTER CAST OF A LOOGIE?

Being made of multiple cells has big advantages. The sponge cells can work together. They can attach themselves in a good position in the water, rather than floating away on the current, which makes it easier to filter food out of the water. Every cell benefits from the presence of the other cells. United, they're stronger. But a collaboration is even better when the cells have their own tasks. A soccer team with a goalkeeper, forwards, and defenders is much more successful than a team made up of only goalies, only forwards, or only defenders. A human with eyes, a nose, a mouth, and a heart is better off than a human with 1,000 eyes, 15 noses, and no mouth at all. It's the same for any living creature with different kinds of cells.

It's better to be an animal with lots of different kinds of cells than a creature with just a few kinds of cells, like the sponge. But how does an animal with different types of cells come about? What were the first examples of such creatures? Hmmm, that's not so easy to find out. You'd need to find fossils of them first, and that's tricky. If you dig up a dinosaur from millions of years ago, you'll never find its heart, its tongue, or its brain. It's always the hard parts that are left behind: bones and teeth. It's the same with shells, because they're just as hard as bones and teeth. That's why we find so many shells that are millions of years old, even though the creatures that once lived inside them died long ago. But the first creatures that lived on Earth didn't have bones or shells. In fact, they were very soft and weak. It would take incredible luck for a creature like that to become a fossil. It'd be like trying to make a plaster cast of a loogie. That's no easy task. But . . . it can be done.

How Does a Jellyfish Become a Fossil?

Imagine some creatures living in shallow water near a volcano. The volcano erupts, hurling millions of pounds of ash into the air. The ash falls into the water, where it covers the creatures, killing them. The layer of ash turns into a kind of mud, and over the course of millions of years, that mud turns into stone. That kind of thing used to happen regularly. The problem is that the fossils are encased within a thick layer of rock, so they aren't visible on the surface. But if the rock is worn away by water, ice, or wind-blown sand, for example, then the fossils can suddenly appear. And that gives us a good idea of how life evolved over millions of years.

WHAT INVENTIONS MADE LIFE TODAY POSSIBLE?

Thanks to the oldest fossils, we know exactly how life developed, from sponge to Joe Schmo from Buffalo. It's as if new "inventions" kept coming along to make life on Earth increasingly sophisticated. Fossils reveal that jellyfish are among the oldest creatures on Earth. Jellyfish have a greater

variety of cells than sponges do but by far not as much as fish, plants, or humans do. Jellyfish have muscle-like tissue that allows them to move, for example.

The first jellyfish were pretty simple. They had no front or back, no brain, and no sense of direction. But over the course of evolution, jellyfish developed something very important: light-sensitive cells. These cells allowed them to tell the difference between light and dark. This was the very beginning of eyes, even though they weren't much like eyes as we know them. That's because we don't just use our eyes to look, but also our brain. And a brain was something the jellyfish didn't have.[17]

How Do You Survive without a Butt?

As time went on, some jellyfish did develop a front and a back. What a breakthrough! Slowly but surely they transformed into flat, elongated creatures: flatworms. These flatworms even had a kind of brain and also light-sensitive cells that allowed them to distinguish between light and dark. That made them the first animals that could really see. And yet jellyfish and flatworms have a problem you wouldn't wish on your worst enemy. Both jellyfish and flatworms eat with the same hole that they poop with, and eating and pooping at the same time is really inconvenient. And it would have to spoil your appetite. But finally some flatworms evolved into worms that were round, like drinking straws, and which could eat with their mouths and poop with their butts. (By the way, a lot of people think you get two worms if you chop an earthworm in half. Nope! Half-worms keep wiggling away for a while, but they die pretty soon. Why? Because earthworms can't survive with just a mouth or just a butt.)

During the age of the single-celled organisms, evolution moved extremely slowly. But after the worms started wiggling their way around the planet, everything started to happen a lot faster. All kinds of new species developed, one after another. One of the reasons for this was that the Earth warmed up. The Earth was really, really cold for millions of years. Some scientists even believe that at one point the Earth must have been one

great big snowball, covered with a layer of ice from the poles to the equator. The only life was in the warmer water beneath that layer of ice and also in the ice itself; lots of bacteria are able to freeze and then just thaw and carry on with their lives as normal. But the Earth becoming warmer was not the most important reason behind this "explosion of the species." That reason was sexual reproduction. But before I tell you more about that, you'll need to know how babies can be born without having two parents involved.

How Can You Be Born without Parents?

No bird, rabbit, or weevil has ever been born without having two parents. But the first life-forms on Earth didn't have parents like we do. Cells like bacteria and archaea just divided, grew, divided again and so on. Animals like some flatworms can use a similar technique. Flatworms split themselves in two—not through the middle but lengthwise so that both halves have a mouth and a butt.[18] Those halves then grow into new, big flatworms. That means that these flatworm babies must be a copy of the parents. How's that for a chip off the old block?

DNA determines what a creature looks like and how it behaves. When an animal reproduces by splitting in two, like the flatworm does, then the "children" have exactly the same DNA. You might think that would make evolution impossible. But that's not the case.

HOW DID THE WORLD GET ITS FIRST MURDERERS?

Take a supersharp photograph of a supersharp photograph. The new photo will look exactly the same as the old one. And now take another photo of that new photo. Again, they're exact copies. Repeat the process 100 times and then compare the last photo with the very first one. What's happened? They're completely different. And yet you can't see any difference between each of the photos and the one before. It's just the same with DNA: every bacterium looks just like its parent. But over the course of time, the DNA sometimes changes a tiny little bit. Tiny mistakes called mutations are introduced during the copying process. Those mistakes are so tiny that you wouldn't notice them. But over hundreds of years they can lead to huge differences. And just imagine what can happen over millions of years!

If you have two parents, those changes start happening much more quickly. You and your mom or your dad don't necessarily end up looking like two peas in a pod. Maybe you have your dad's long nose or your mom's upturned nose or something in between. Remember the part in this book earlier about genes, ants, and information? All the ant sisters had the same genes, the same information. That's why they all looked alike. You have half of the genes of your dad or mom, a quarter of each of your grandparents, and an eighth of each of your great-grandparents. So all kinds of differences can happen much more quickly.

Twenty-Six Peanut Butter and Jelly Sandwiches, Anyone?

So, once there were parents, there were huge numbers of new species. That was just the beginning of an explosion of even more new species, ones with fins, muscles, or tentacles to propel themselves forward. The newcomers were more and more active. And if you move a lot, you're constantly using energy. An average human adult male needs around 2,500 calories a day. That's seven peanut butter and jelly sandwiches. A cyclist on a difficult race day needs as many as 9,000 calories. That's 26 peanut butter and jelly sandwiches.[19] Moving certainly makes a difference. The first animals on Earth didn't move

very quickly at all. They had only three speeds: slow, really slow, and standing still. A simple snack was enough for them. But it was a completely different story for the newcomers. They had to search for the food with the highest nutritional value. Which food contained the most energy? A couple of lettuce leaves give you just a few calories. That was more than enough for the first creatures; they could get by on plants for food. But the new animals really needed something more. Plants and algae weren't enough. To get all the energy they needed, they ate . . . other animals. They were the first murderers! Or rather: the first predators. Meat protein contains a lot more calories than vegetable matter. To get 100 calories, you have to eat two large heads of lettuce. But just a couple of ounces of steak contain the same number of calories. A horse has to eat hours and hours a day to eat up to 25 pounds of grass, while a few pounds of meat are enough for a much smaller lion.[20]

WHAT WOULD A ZOO HAVE LOOKED LIKE 550 MILLION YEARS AGO?

Predators had a massive influence on the speed of evolution. Which predators had the greatest chance of survival? The fastest, the best, and the most dangerous. And what prey had the greatest chance of survival? The ones with the best camouflage, defense, or protection. That's natural selection at work again. And so, the predators kept getting faster, better, and more dangerous, while prey animals developed all kinds of different defensive techniques. This resulted in many completely new animals.

Imagine there was a zoo back then (or actually, a big aquarium, because everyone still lived in the water at that time). What animals would you have seen there? Well, animals like these, for example, some of which are still around:

AQUARIUM

550,000,000 YEARS BCE

1. Opabinia

This was a bizarre little predator around three inches long, with five eyes. Its murder weapon was a grappling claw at the end of its proboscis.[21]

2. Wiwaxia

One of the first creatures with protective scales and spines, it ranged from just one-eigth to two inches in length.[22]

3. Kimberella

Scientists are still debating whether this is more like a jellyfish or perhaps a mollusk, like a slug. It is neither but something in between. What makes this creature remarkable is that it had a kind of shell. Not a hard one, like a crab's shell or a seashell, but a soft and flexible one.[23]

4. Holothuria

Peculiar, soft creatures with a really weird defensive technique. When in danger, they start to poop. And they just keep on pooping. Even after all of the poop has left their bodies, they still go on pooping. They poop out their insides! Any predator chasing stares in amazement and then gobbles up the innards. *Holothuria* live without their intestines for a while until they grow back. (How do we know all this, by the way? They're still alive and pooping: we call them sea cucumbers!)[24]

5. Hallucigenia

What kind of creature was this one? The experts couldn't figure it out. It had two rows of legs and funny tentacle thingies on its back. It looked like nothing on Earth. So, scientists called it *Hallucigenia*—after *hallucinations*, the weird visions that people can have. Then what happened? They found out that they'd been looking at the creature upside down. The "legs" were actually protective spines on its back, and the tentacle thingies were actually its legs.[25]

6. Spriggina

This was an ultramodern creature for that time. It had a head and a tail. It may have even had eyes. It could have been the first creature that could see its food before it took a bite. So, it could also be the first animal that lost its appetite.[26]

7. Anomalocaris

This fossil also presented scientists with a puzzle. They found some weird creatures and had absolutely no idea how they worked. It wasn't until later that they figured it out: these weren't different animals but parts of one monster that was over three feet long. Its giant limbs in front looked a lot like shrimp tails and were used to grab prey.[27]

Hunting and defending. Hunting and dodging. Hunting and hiding. An arms race began between the predators and their prey, which is still going on today. The predators acquired weapons (sharp teeth and claws); the prey got spines and armor. These shields not only made them safer but also made their bodies more robust. Armor and shells held those soft bodies together. Because of the predators, the prey evolved into much more useful forms. The herrings of today should be grateful to the sharks of the past. And vice versa . . .

WHAT WAS THE MOST SUCCESSFUL CREATURE OF THE PAST?

Sturdy shells don't just develop out of nowhere. But even though they're so useful to the creature inside, they actually came into existence by accident. The first shellfish were completely defenseless. But they had help from their daily diet. These creatures ate food that contained lots of calcium and minerals. They couldn't easily get rid of the hard parts of these substances, so they ended up on the outside of their bodies.[28] And the more there was, the better protection they had, and the easier it was for them to survive.

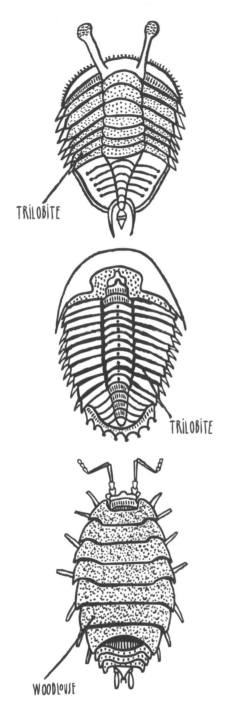

TRILOBITE

TRILOBITE

WOODLOUSE

The only problem with a shell is its weight: shellfish have to keep to the seabed. But the nautiloids came up with a solution. These squid-like creatures had a straight or coiled shell that they could fill with gas so that it floated in the water, just like a balloon. When they wanted to go back down again, they pumped in some water. That's a really handy way for a predator to get to anywhere it wants to go. It made these creatures very powerful indeed. Some of them grew to be monsters that were eight feet in length.[29] No creature on Earth could defeat these killing machines; the only creatures that stood a chance against nautiloids were ammonites. But then they were very similar to nautiloids.

Who Wiped Out the Trilobite?

A hard, solid shell is great for defense. But armor that can move with your body is a lot more useful. We call creatures with these kinds of shells arthropods. Their flexible armor made the arthropods just as successful as the nautiloids and ammonites. They came in all shapes and sizes, from tiny to gigantic. The oceans were teeming with these little beasties, bigger beasts, and monsters. They still are, in fact. Shrimps, lobsters, spiders, and wood lice are all arthropods. Some live in the ocean, some on land. But there was once another group of underwater arthropods, one that lived 520 million years ago: the trilobites. Trilobites looked a bit like wood lice, but they sometimes grew longer than two feet.

Thousands of trilobite fossils have been found. Not just because they appeared in huge quantities, but also because their armor meant they could leave behind a nice imprint. That's how we know so much about them. Some trilobites had pretty good eyes for the time. Some crawled through the mud and couldn't see a thing. Other mud trilobites knew exactly what was going on above them, because their eyes were on stalks. There were other trilobites that had no eyes at all. They lived at such a depth that none of them could see anything anyway because the sunlight didn't reach that far. The trilobites were among the most successful animals on Earth, and yet they suddenly died out. It's still a big mystery how that happened, because these creatures had everything going for them. They were a little like the most successful group of animals today: the insects. You could even call them the precursors of the insects. But underwater insects, of course.

FROM WHICH SEA CREATURE ARE WE DESCENDED?

The trilobites of all those many years ago had a great deal in common with the insects of today. But which creature of the past do we humans have most in common with? From which animal are we descended? Those lethal nautiloids? From the superdeadly *Anomalocaris*? It can't be one of those sluggish *Kimberella*, can it? No, it's much worse: our closest relative is a tunicate.

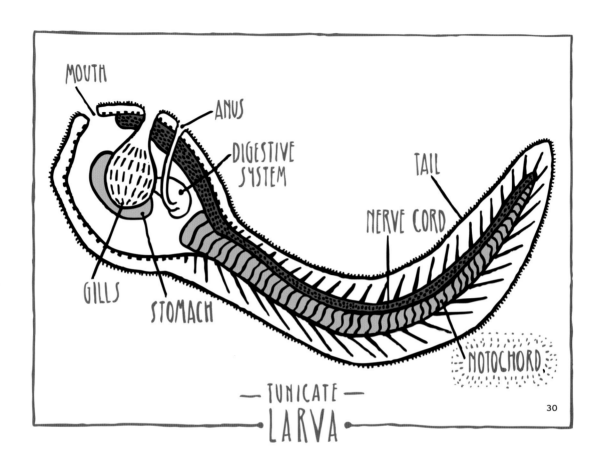

MOUTH

ANUS

DIGESTIVE SYSTEM

TAIL

NERVE CORD

GILLS

STOMACH

NOTOCHORD

— TUNICATE —
LARVA

30

A what? Tunicates look a lot like wobbly bags of Jell-O. And we share 80 percent of our genes with these completely insignificant little creatures that have been living in the seas for about 500 million years.[31]

When you look at adult tunicates, also called sea squirts, that seems impossible. And yet the larvae have something that we human beings also have: a notochord. Well, we had one when our embryos were four weeks old. Later it disappeared and helped form our backbone.[32] When the creatures become adults, the backbone can no longer be seen, but it's still visible when they're young. Our backbone is one of the most important parts of our body. So our ancestor is a kind of flabby test tube. If you were being kind, you might say it looks a bit like a flower. But it gets worse: some tunicates evolved into hagfish.[33] And if that name weren't bad enough, they're sometimes known as slime eels! We have even more in common with those slimy beasts than notochords.

Were Our Ancestors Slime Balls?

Slime eels . . . As the name suggests, hagfish are far and away the slimiest creatures on Earth. They're long, jawless fish that protect themselves by producing huge quantities of slime when they're in danger. The slime swells up to form a thick, protective layer when it comes into contact with water. Just one of these creatures can turn the water in a big bucket into such thick goop that you could turn the bucket upside down and it wouldn't fall out. And yep, that's our ancestor from 400 million years ago. But there's good news too. It's also the ancestor of the first real fish—the fish with jaws. So *they're* even closer relatives. It could be worse.

Shellfish, snails, and arthropods all have their skeletons on the outside. But fish, birds, reptiles, and mammals have their bones on the inside. That's much more practical when you want to move. This new design produced the most lethal predator that ever lived in the sea: the megalodon. This was a kind of shark that made the waters a very dangerous place for hundreds of millions of years. It became extinct around 2 million years ago, and we can be thankful that it did.[34] This beast was the size of a bus—sometimes bigger!—and had a mouth the size of a whiteboard. It could have gulped down a whole cow in one bite, without chewing.

We have quite a lot in common with those sharks. They're among the oldest fish on Earth. And we are descended from them too. If you look carefully, you can see that we're still very fishy creatures.

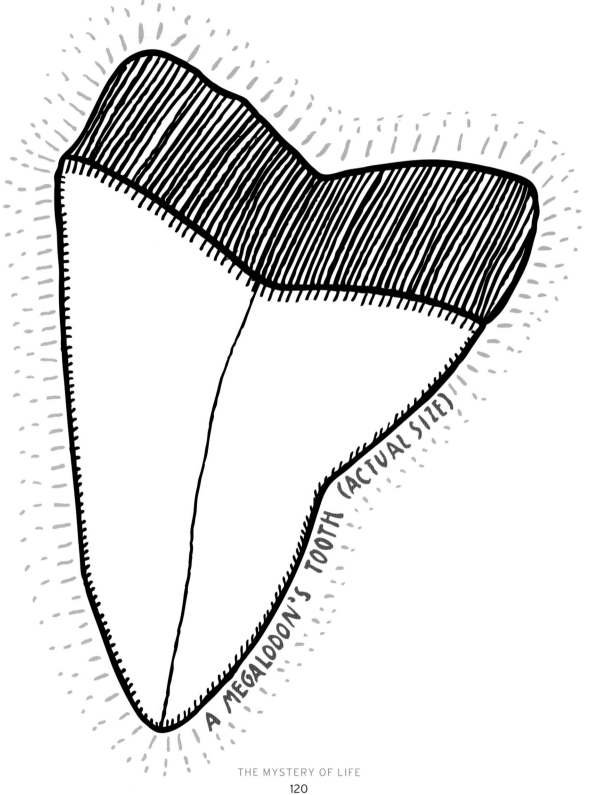

A MEGALODON'S TOOTH (ACTUAL SIZE)

CHAPTER 9

Half Human, Half Fish

HOW DOES A FISH GET FOUR LEGS?

After the move from nonliving to living, the shift from sea to land is just about the biggest change ever to happen on Earth. It's no wonder it took billions of years before some sea creatures (and plants) felt ready to exchange the safety of the water for the land and the air. Scientists think that land plants had evolved on Earth by about 700 million years ago and land fungi by about 1,300 million years ago.[1] With plants, it's pretty easy to imagine how it happened. Some plants still live half in the water and half above. It's no problem with slugs, snails, and worms either. They live in the sea and on the land, and the sea versions are practically identical to the land versions. And when you think that a wood louse breathes through gills, it's hardly surprising that it's descended from a sea creature.[2] It's actually just a modern trilobite.

Is a Fish with Lungs a Big Deal?

But what about us? The mammals? How do you change from a fish into a quadruped, a creature with four legs? That's a different story. You only have to visit the fish counter at your local supermarket to see the biggest problem that fish have to contend with when they end up on dry land. Fish can't breathe in the air. Fish have gills, not lungs. Unlike wood lice, fish clearly can't breathe out of the water. That's why trout, salmon, mackerel, and just about every other fish you know don't survive very long once they're out of the water. For the first scientists who studied evolution, the transition from sea to land was a big mystery. That was until, in 1831, scientists working in South America encountered a very strange fish indeed: a fish with lungs![3] Soon after that, these lungfish were also found in Africa and Australia. These very special creatures partly solved the mystery. Well, I'm making it sound like lungfish are a big deal, but that didn't stop people serving them up for dinner.

How Do Gills Become Lungs?

But what good are lungs to a fish? And how do gills suddenly change into lungs? The answer is: they don't. Lungfish have both gills and lungs. They can breathe in the water and out of the water. But where did those lungs come from? They developed from an important organ that many fish use: the swim bladder. Fast fish like tuna are always on the move; when they want to go up or down, they simply swim in that direction. Other fish are pretty heavy, so they're always to be found down at the bottom of the water. And then there are the fish that use their swim bladder. It's a kind of balloon inside their body that they can pump up with oxygen when they want to move upward. Oxygen's lighter than water. The bigger the "balloon" is, the faster these fish can get to the top. When they want to go back down, they simply pump out some of the oxygen. It's a very handy thing, a swim bladder. In some fish, that useful organ later evolved into lungs.[4]

So, Where Did the Legs Come From?

Now we know how fish got lungs. But what about the legs? How did fins change into feet? The answer to this question can be seen in the same fish. Some fish like lungfish have unusual fins, too. There are two on one side, and two on the other side. So they're just like front legs and back legs. And some of them actually use their fins to walk. They usually do so in the water, but lungfish can even use their "legs" to cross land.[5]

No matter how good a lungfish is at walking on dry land, it's still a fish. And a fish lives in the water. That's where lungfish are most at home. Amphibians aren't fish. They need the land in order to survive. Fishes have scales, amphibians have moist skin. And fishes use their gills to obtain oxygen, while amphibians use their lungs. Amphibians and fish are completely different kinds of animals. There must once have been some kind of "missing link" between fish and amphibians walking and swimming around. If that's true, then we should be able to find fossils of that creature. But do such fossils exist?

PLEASE ACCEPT MY HUMBLE APOLOGIES

Well, I'd have liked to have jumped right in and started talking about the fossils that bridge the gap between the fish and the amphibians. But instead I'll first have to tell you something different—and offer my humble apologies. In the chapter about the age of the Earth, I wrote about how geologists once worked out how old layers of rock were. I said they used fossils to do it. But that's not the whole story. Not at all. Because the age of the fossils was determined by the rock where they were found. Another chicken-and-egg problem! To work out the age of the fossils, scientists used the type of rock . . . and to work out the age of the rock, they used—that's right—fossils.[6] It's like trying set your watch by a clock at the same time as you're trying to set the clock by your watch. But working out the age was not an impossible task.

Why Do We Use Fossils to Write on Blackboards?

Determining the age of rocks and fossils is like a jigsaw puzzle with lots and lots of different pieces. The deeper you dig, the older the layer. So the depth of the layer is already a clue to its age. The type of rock also contains a lot of information about the past. Take chalk, for example. On the French and English coasts, there are large chalk cliffs. Chalk is made up of the shells of minuscule sea creatures. Those shells sank down to the bottom of the ocean, and more shells landed on top of them, and more, and more, and so on. Yes, when you write on a blackboard, you're actually writing with fossils that are hundreds of millions years old. But those huge chalk cliffs tell us that incredibly long ago there was a sea in that place, one that entirely covered those chalk cliffs.

It's obvious that a layer of chalk that's 300 feet high in places can't have formed in a weekend. Millions of years were needed. If you find a fossil at the bottom of a really thick layer of chalk, you know it has to be millions and millions of years old. Every kind of rock has its own secrets to reveal, as does every kind of fossil. At one point in time, the Earth was swarming with trilobites. That's why we've found so many of them. But those trilobites are only to be found in very old layers of stone, because they became extinct long ago. If you find a fossil of a trilobite and a fossil of a shark in the same layer, you know that sharks already existed in the days of the trilobites. Maybe the sharks even played a part in making the trilobites extinct by eating them up.

If You Dig Deep Enough, Will You Automatically Find Fossils?

By combining all of these details about fossils and layers of rock, you can make a nice timeline of all of the species that have been discovered as fossils. In the oldest and deepest layers, there are no traces of living creatures. A little higher, you can find the first jellyfish and flatworms. Then come the crustaceans, and so on. Until you get to the mammals of today. But don't go thinking you can find a spot where the entire process of evolution runs neatly from the bottom to the top. Fossils form only in very special circumstances. That's what makes them so remarkable. The probability of fossils forming in one single place over hundreds of millions of years and stacking up like cards in a deck is extremely small. You need to compare layers of earth from all over the world in order to solve the puzzle.

Not only that, but the world's far too busy moving around. Moving? Yes. The Earth doesn't stand still. Without realizing, you're very slowly sliding in a certain direction.

WHY DO YOU FIND THE SAME KIND OF ROCKS IN THE AMERICAS AND AFRICA?

There's another puzzle piece that holds information about the age of rocks and fossils: the Earth itself! If you look at the Earth as it is now, you can see that you'd have to fly or sail a really long way to get from Africa to America. But there was a time when it was possible to swim that distance. And at one point, you could even jump it! The continents once lay right next to each other—if you look carefully, you can see that the eastern part of South America fits neatly into the western part of Africa.[8] The layers of rock are the same too. If you dig down 60, 300, or 600 feet, you'll find exactly the same rock in eastern Brazil and western Cameroon. It's like cutting a layer cake in two.

Did Palm Trees Once Grow in the Polar Regions?

The continents shift because the crust of the Earth is divided into lots of different pieces, called plates. And underground forces in the Earth are what make those pieces move. That means that, every day, Africa and the Americas move a little farther apart. This is an excruciatingly slow process, by the way. It happens at about the same speed a fingernail grows. (So you can imagine how long those continents have been moving apart.) There are also parts that move back toward each other again so that one plate shifts beneath another. Other plates rub up against each other. You notice it right away when that happens. Alarm systems go off, animals make loud noises, and buildings start to shake: that's an earthquake.

The Earth is billions of years old, so the continents once looked very different indeed. Sections of the polar regions were once located at the equator and vice versa. We can work out exactly which continent was once where.

PERMIAN

JURASSIC

CRETACEOUS

NOW!

[9]

And that gives us more new information. If you find fossils of reptiles and palm trees in the far north, you know those fossils must have been there for hundreds of millions of years. From the time when that place was closer to the equator. Or from a time when the Earth was a lot warmer. Greenland, for example, has been in the north for a very long time, but the Earth was so warm that palm trees could grow even there, close to the North Pole.[10]

So we can get a lot of information about how old things are from Earth's changes in temperature—from the ice ages to the periods when the Earth was one big hothouse.

How Old Is *Tyrannosaurus rex*'s Footprint?

Just a couple of puzzle pieces aren't much help. But if you put all of the pieces together, you can get a clear picture of what a place on Earth looked like during a particular era. Scientists are able to combine all of the puzzle pieces and information. If you don't know how old a certain rock is, but you find a *Tyrannosaurus rex* footprint in it, then you know that layer has to be around 70 million years old. We also know about the half-life of radioactive elements, which gives an even better indication of which era rocks and fossils come from. So a lot of the puzzle has already been solved.

Phew. Anyway, now you understand why I couldn't just throw in all that information about the age of rocks in a couple of quick sentences. But you need to know this in order to understand how a fish was once able to change into a quadruped, so I thought I'd better give you a quick explanation.

WHERE DO YOU FIND THE FINEST FOSSILS?

Okay, the deeper you dig, the farther back in time you go. The finest and oldest fossils are hidden deep beneath immense layers of earth and rocks. But that doesn't mean you can't find stones on the surface that are hundreds of millions of years old. Some layers of rock wear away, as vast quantities of sand blow across them every day, which has the effect of sandpaper. That's what happens in the Moroccan desert, for example.[11] You can find the most wonderful fossils there, just lying around. On the east coast of Canada, the rocks have been worn away by waves, wind, ice, and smaller stones.[12] There's a huge number of unusual fossils there too. Other rocks have been pushed all the way up to the surface as mountains formed. That's why you can suddenly come across an imprint of a sea snail or a shell up in the mountains. Even on the summits of the Himalayas![13]

How Do You Go About Finding an Amphibish or a Fishphibian?

When you know where to look, you have a much better chance of finding what you're looking for. Good paleontologists—that's what people who study fossils are called—never just start digging in the hope that they might find something. They first make a thorough study of the ground and the conditions. The paleontologist Neil Shubin used all of the available knowledge when he went in search of the fossil of an unknown creature that was half amphibian, half fish.[14] This missing fossil was extremely import-ant. Fish that were similar to amphibians had already been found, such as *Panderichthys*.[15] With a bit of imagination, you can see the head of a frog and the legs of a turtle on this fish. It also had a long tail that seemed quite unlike a fish's tail. Its fins had bones that were just like fingers, but it was still a fish. *Acanthostega* came from a later period. It was an excellent swim-mer, so spent most of its time in the water. It was like a kind of eel with legs. But it was most definitely an amphibian.[16] Something in between the two had never been found, and that was what Shubin was looking for: conclu-sive proof that amphibians evolved from fish. But . . . how do you go about finding something like that?

What Do You Need if You Want to Find Fossils?

Shubin knew that three ingredients were necessary to find a particular sort of fossil. You can use the same ingredients yourself if you ever go hunting for fossils. First, you have to look inside rocks of the right age. Second, you need the sort of rocks that can contain fossils. And third, you have to be very—no, make that very, very—lucky!

The first ingredient was easy to work out, for Shubin. The fossils of the fishlike amphibians and the amphibian-like fish were around 375 and 380 million years old. For his fossil, Shubin had to go looking for rock that was somewhere around these ages. You can look on the internet nowadays to find out where this kind of stone occurs. That's what Shubin does too.

The second ingredient wasn't too tricky to arrange either. There's no point investigating rocks that were once molten lava, for instance. No fossil can survive at the temperature of liquid stone. But other layers of rock, such as limestone or sandstone, are suitable. Again, you can look on the internet to see where exactly you can find these kinds of rocks. Shubin discovered three large areas with exactly the right kind of stone. The first was in a spot with lots of buildings. It's difficult to dig beneath a parking garage, so that was out. The second was in a region that had been thoroughly studied by paleontologists. The chance of Shubin finding something there that everyone else had overlooked was slim. So he knew not to start searching there either. But the third region was a vast plain near the North Pole, where no one ever went. Shubin knew that was the place to go!

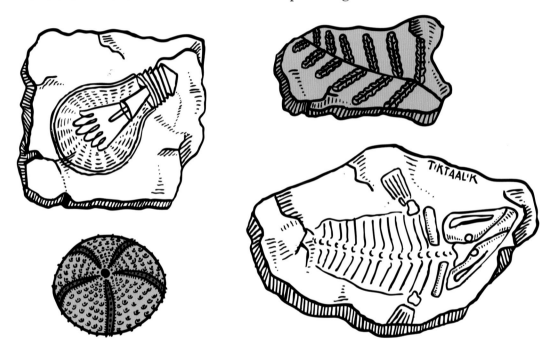

So . . . ? Was the Fossil of Fossils Ever Found?

That close to the North Pole, it freezes almost all year round. Shubin could only go there in the summer, when the temperature was around 50 degrees Fahrenheit. In those few weeks, he had to search for a creature in an area of hundreds of square miles. That's why the third ingredient is so important: without a good deal of luck, you'll never find a fossil like that.

Shubin was proved right: there are plenty of fossils in the polar region. Unfortunately, most of them are fossils of deep-sea fish. And an animal that lived partly on the land and partly in the sea must, of course, have been in shallower water. After his first search, Shubin returned home with lots of fossils, but they weren't the fossil he was looking for. The same happened the next year. And the year after that. But in 2004, on his fourth expedition, he came across a creature with a flat head like a crocodile, scales like a fish, a neck like an amphibian—good—fins like a fish, and—yes!—ribs like an amphibian! Shubin had found what he was looking for: the animal that was not a fish and not an amphibian but both. He called it *Tiktaalik roseae*, which is the name of a kind of large freshwater fish in the language of the Inuit, the people who live in the North Pole region.

Shubin had found his definitive proof that amphibians evolved from fish.

HOW IS JOE SCHMO LIKE A SHARK?

Different specimens of *Tiktaalik* have since been found, including one that was almost 10 feet long. But how closely do we resemble this "fishphibian" of 383 million years ago?[17] Perhaps more closely than you might think.

Does Joe Schmo from Buffalo Have *Tiktaalik*'s Arm?

The fish that would eventually evolve into amphibians had a special feature, something that all amphibians, reptiles, birds, and mammals share. If you compare Tiktaalik's front fins with Joe Schmo from Buffalo's arm, you'll see exactly the same structure.

Joe Schmo's arm (and your arm too) starts with a large upper-arm bone, the humerus. At the elbow, it turns into two bones: the ulna and the

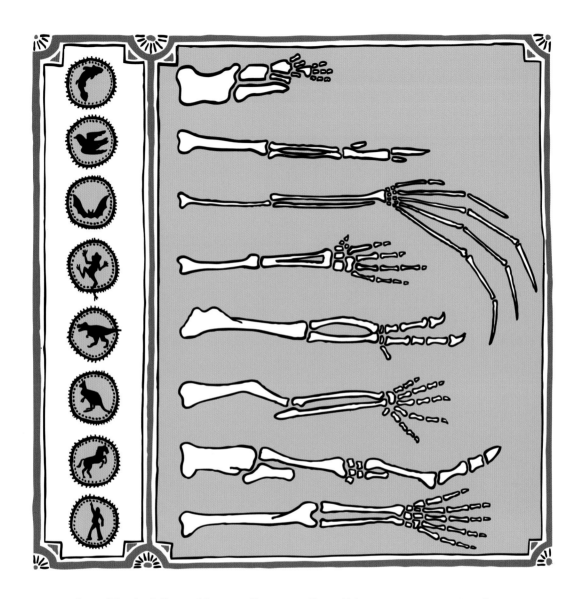

radius. That's followed by a collection of small bones in your wrist, known as the carpal bones. Finally, there are the bones in the hand and the fingers: the metacarpals and the phalanges. And here it comes: all of the creatures that descended from *Tiktaalik* and his kind have the same structure in their "arms"—from bird to bat, from *Tyrannosaurus rex* to turtledove, and from frog to kangaroo. Each has a front leg or wing that begins with one bone, which is followed by two bones, and then the leg continues in the form of a cluster of small bones, which in turn are followed by something resembling finger bones.

Why Is a Horse's Hoof like a Human's Hand?

The structure of large land animals is the same everywhere. Of course, the form and size are completely different; you can't expect a bat to fly if it has the front legs of an elephant. A bat's "arm" is very different even from a bird's. A bat's wing is actually one big hand with extremely long, thin "finger" bones. A bird has few such bones, and their length is much shorter than a bat's. Most of the wing consists of feathers without bone. In horses, some of the bones have become much larger, while others have practically disappeared. The horse's hoof is actually the equivalent of your middle fingernail! In frogs, other bones have fused and lengthened, so that they look absolutely nothing like a horse's front leg. But the basic structure is exactly the same. Even *Acanthostega* from 360 million years ago has legs with exactly the same structure as Joe Schmo's arm.

Do We Hear with Shark Gills?

If you wind the evolutionary clock back, you can see that arm structure disappearing. Going back in time, more and more fish bones are made from cartilage, not bone. Fish today have bones that have disappeared in humans, and we also have some bones that they don't. We have ribs to protect our heart and our lungs from hard knocks. Fish never needed those bones in the water. And yet you'll find quite a few similarities between humans and sharks. We humans no longer have gills, but the remnants of gills are still inside our heads.

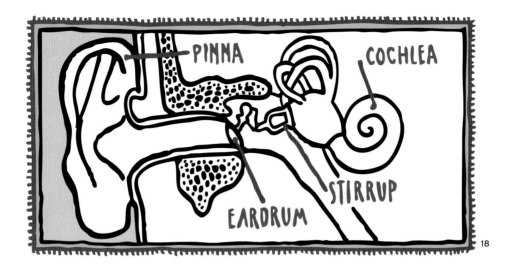

One of the bones inside our middle ear that help us to hear comes from a fish's gill, for instance. In humans, it's a tiny little bone (the stapes, or stirrup bone), but sharks still have a huge chunk of cartilage. And if you compare that bone in sharks, modern fish, amphibians, reptiles, and human beings, you can see exactly what happened during the process of evolution. With each more modern class of animals, the bone has become smaller, finally ending up as a minuscule bone inside the human ear.

HOW WERE YOU ONCE LIKE A MACKEREL?

Not everyone believes in evolution. Many people still believe that God completed the Earth in six days, along with everything on it. And one of the arguments these people often use is that something as complex as a human being could never have evolved from a single-celled creature. Not even in billions of years. Science's answer is simple: "Impossible? You think so? But didn't you develop from a single cell yourself? In fact, it took you just nine months to grow from a cell into a human being!"

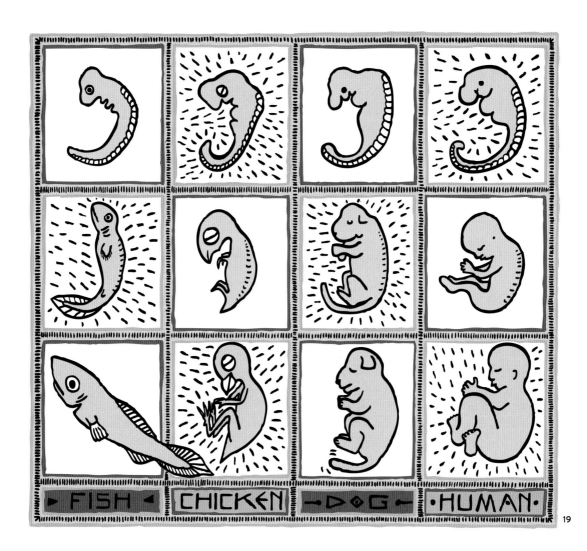

FISH · CHICKEN · DOG · HUMAN

19

Why Do All Creatures Start Out Alike?

The scientific answer is, of course, right. We are indeed complex creatures. Our bodies are like machines that perform around a million tasks a minute to keep us alive—and without us ever thanking them for all that hard work, incidentally. And no matter how ingenious our bodies are, every single one of us began life as a tiny, single-celled little thing. But when you think about this answer for a while, it actually starts to sound a little weak. We can only grow from a cell to a human being because our DNA makes sure that we do. And a DNA molecule is a hugely complex thing. So complex that you could easily think it must have been designed by a god.

And yet, in actual fact, science is even more right than it seemed at first. Because that period before our birth perfectly demonstrates the process of evolution. The farther we look back into our own past, the more closely we resemble other animals. Right at the beginning, when we're made of just one cell, there's no difference at all. Every fertilized egg looks the same, whether it's a bird, an elephant, or a fish. When it divides from one cell into two, from two to four, to eight, sixteen, thirty-two, and more and more, you can still see a cluster of identical cells. Two weeks after that, the first different cells start to form. Some become a heart, while others turn into brains, intestines, or muscles. One to two weeks later, the heart has already started beating, but the human still looks just like birds, fish, and reptiles do at that stage.[20] It actually seems as if the human is well on the way to becoming a fish . . .

Why Do Your Ears Pop When You Descend in an Elevator?

Believe it or not, you once looked a lot like a mackerel. It was about eight months before you were born. The place where your eyes were going to be was still at the side of your head, just like a mackerel. It wasn't until later that your eyes shifted to the front. You had a long tail; all you needed to do was glue on a tailfin and you could have swum around like a fish. And then clearly visible "gill arches" grew near your head. In fish, these arches become slits that open up to allow in water. But in humans, they should close up. Very rarely a child is born with rudiments of gill arch cartilage, and the child has to have surgery. That's one of the disadvantages of having a fish as an ancestor.[21]

You can also notice your fishy ancestry when you're in an airplane or an elevator that's going up quickly. If you yawn in an elevator, you may feel your ears popping. That's because you have a tube inside your head by your ear. In fish, it's the gill opening, which they use to let in water. In humans, this evolved into the Eustachian tube.[22] The difference in elevation causes a change in the air pressure in your head. When you yawn, the tube opens for a moment, and the pressure becomes normal again.[23]

Why Does Tweety Have Such a Big Head?

Eventually, of course, you change into a creature that's completely different from a fish and looks more and more like a human baby. And evolution can be seen there too. Embryos—that's what animals are called in the first stages of development in an egg or mother's womb—first look a

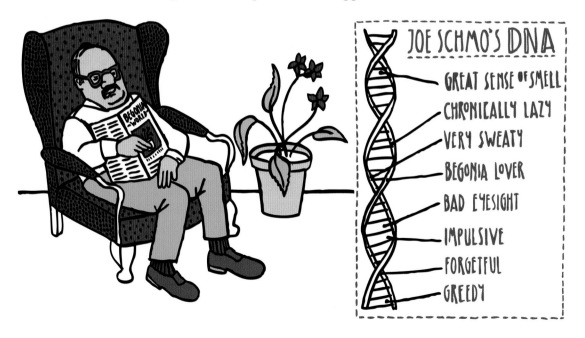

bit like a fish. After a few weeks the differences become bigger between fishes, amphibians, birds, and mammals. In the final stage, a clear difference between birds and humans also becomes apparent. It's not until the very end of the process that humans and other mammals start to look less like one another. The most important difference is that we have an enormous brain and larger head compared to our body size than other mammals. Only birds have a head that's comparatively as large, but there's a different reason for that. In birds, the head isn't larger because of the brain, but because of the big eyes, which take up most of the head.[24]

HOW DOES A CELL KNOW WHETHER TO BECOME A TOOTH, A NOSE, OR A TOE?

It's not only in evolution that we started out as a fish. We also spend the very first days of our existence as "fish." The changes don't happen until later in the development of our cells. But how does that happen? How does a cell know whether to become a hand, a paw, or a fin? Or a brain cell or a heart muscle? It's because of our DNA. It contains all of the secrets of our existence. That six-foot-long DNA molecule contains all the information to make Joe Schmo from Buffalo Joe Schmo from Buffalo and a begonia a begonia.

What Could You Compare DNA To?

It's difficult to compare DNA to anything. DNA's a bit like a general giving orders to an army of Joe Schmo cells or begonia cells. But a few chapters ago, I compared the DNA to a construction kit with instructions explaining exactly how to build a Joe Schmo or a begonia. And to a recipe from a cookbook for a Joe Schmo, Buffalo style, or begonia à la potted plant. But you can also see DNA as a machine. A machine that transforms substances into bones, flesh and limbs, leaves, roots, and flowers. Or a computer program: "Make cell. Duplicate cell. After 20 duplications, make new cells. Repeat." None of these comparisons is a perfect fit, but they're all a little bit true.

DNA contains rules for a cell to follow. It contains all of the commands that a cell has to perform. It contains a complete blueprint for a living creature or the recipe needed to "cook" one. And it knows all the techniques for building the necessary cells, changing them, killing them, and disposing of them.

Can the Cells in Your Body Talk to One Another?

The most important elements of your DNA are your genes, those short pieces of information on the DNA molecule. The genes decide if you're going to have brown or blue eyes, if you'll have skin or feathers, and if you'll consist of one cell, like a slipper animalcule, or 37.2 trillion cells, like a person. Genes have a kind of on-and-off switch. They use it to turn on and off instructions such as "use amino acids to make this protein" or "break down this

GRIPE · DNA
— 3 TIMES A DAY —
AGE 30 AND UP

protein." Using lots and lots of commands like this, they can build exactly the right kind of cell that's required in a particular place. The DNA knows exactly where it needs to turn these genes off and on. This is because the cells can use protein molecules to "talk" to one another.

Put simply, cells use proteins to send molecules to one another in order to exchange information. There are several kinds of molecules by which proteins can communicate. For instance some of these signal molecules are called hormones, and they determine things like whether you grow up to be a man or a woman. Other signal molecules can be neurotransmitters. These neurotransmitters communicate between nerve cells and help you feel the pain when a bowling ball drops on your toes. The signal molecules contain information, and they "tell" the receiver proteins who they all are and what they have to do or become.[25] This kind of information exchange by sending molecules is, of course, different from the way humans communicate. After receiving a molecule, the receiver protein might change or react. The DNA in a cell determines in which way the proteins react or respond. Based on information from nearby cells, the DNA decides, for example, that the proteins should react to form a cell into a skin cell, that it needs to split in two, or that it should stay as it is. And so cells can grow together into a begonia or a Joe Schmo. And not only that, but they also make sure your finger heals when you cut yourself. They discover that there's a wound and then make sure that substances are released to clot the blood and that new skin cells grow to seal up the wound.

How Do You Make a Fly with Extra Wings?

Scientists are very curious about all of the information in our genes and our DNA. They're nowhere near knowing the exact purpose of every gene. But their research has already revealed a great deal, particularly through experiments with embryos. For example, they attached a fruit fly's wing-making genes to a completely different part of the embryo fly's body. And what happened? The fly grew extra wings in that spot.[26] They cut the cells from a freshly laid salamander egg in two. And what happened? Two perfectly healthy, completely normal salamanders were born.[27]

Scientists don't mess around with genes and embryos for the fun of it. This work has an important purpose. The knowledge that these researchers have gained has made it possible for us to grow human body parts from cells. There are already people walking around with a new bladder or skin tissue that was grown in a lab.[28]

WHAT CAN A VIRUS TELL US ABOUT OUR PAST?

DNA is not only useful for doctors who want to grow new skin or a bladder for their patients. It's also a good way to see evolution. We can't find DNA in old fossils, because there's none left after all that time. In perfect circumstances, DNA can survive for a few thousand years, but that happens only rarely.[29] But you can use the DNA of living creatures. It's very simple. Your DNA is most similar to your parents' DNA. It's also very similar to your grandparents' but slightly less so. The farther back in time you go, the greater the differences between us and our ancestors. When there are more differences, there must also be more differences in the DNA. So, the more our DNA resembles someone else's, the more closely we are related.

The DNA of chimpanzees and bonobos, for example, is very similar to our own, almost 99 percent, in fact.[30] That proves that we're very close in evolutionary terms. We share around 90 percent of our DNA with a cat. And 60 percent of our DNA is the same as a fruit fly's. You can take it even further: large chunks of our DNA are the same as the DNA of jellyfish, trees, fungi, and bacteria.[31]

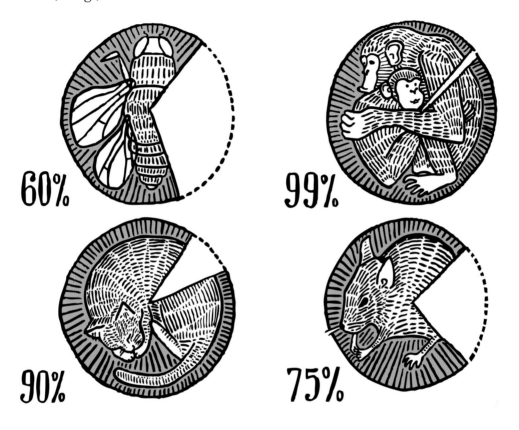

60%   99%

90%   75%

What Can a Sneezing Fit Nine Feet Away Do to Us?

There's another way to see how distant we are from different animals, and it's just as handy as DNA. We can do it with retroviruses. It works like this. You've almost certainly had the flu at some point. The flu is caused by a virus. Viruses are small and nasty pieces of DNA wrapped in protein. They find their way into your body when you come into contact with someone who already has the virus. The sick person sneezes in your direction, within nine feet of you. Because that's how far a person can sneeze. You breathe in the virus molecules—and whoosh: the virus takes up residence in your DNA. If it's a dangerous virus, it can make you really sick or even kill you.

A retrovirus is similar to a virus. The biggest difference is that it is made not of DNA but of RNA. A retrovirus inserts itself into the DNA of your cells and takes over. It changes the DNA and hops from one cell to the next. Which is, of course, deadly dangerous if these changes make you sick. Retroviruses are a great enemy of every living creature. HIV is one example of a retrovirus that's killed many people. Luckily, you can't catch viruses like HIV from a sneezing fit.[32]

Did Apes Have the Same Flu as Us?

Retroviruses have been around for millions of years. But they don't kill every creature that they infect. Some animals find a way to survive. They just go on living with the retroviruses in their bodies. And so do their offspring. The retroviruses don't do any more damage, but they've changed their DNA and the DNA of all of their descendants forever.

We can look for those retroviruses in our DNA and see which animals have the same retroviruses. And what does this reveal? Chimpanzees often carry the same retroviruses as us. Humans and chimps share many of the ancestors who survived these diseases. We share fewer retroviruses with gorillas. And even fewer with baboons, which are not apes but a closely related species. So scientists can tell that humans are more closely related to chimpanzees than to gorillas or baboons.[33]

WHY IS A COW MORE LIKE A WHALE THAN LIKE A HORSE?

The more distant from us an animal is in evolutionary terms, the fewer retroviruses we share and the more different our DNA is. It's also possible to compare the DNA of other animals to see how closely they're related. This provides absolutely fascinating information. Would you like an example? Dogs are descended from wolves. Everyone knows that. But there's a Japanese breed of dog called the shiba inu that looks more like a fox than a wolf. Why should they be descended from wolves and not foxes? Wouldn't that make more sense? But research into their DNA has proven that this dog also has the wolf as its ancestor. That's true not just for the shiba inu but for every dog out there.[34]

Another example: Who do you think is more closely related: a cow and a horse or a cow and a whale? If you think it's a cow and a horse, you'd be wrong. The whale and the cow are distant "cousins," but cows and horses are even more distantly related. Whales, cows, hippopotamuses, and sheep have the same ancestor.[35] The evidence was first found by comparing their DNA.

It wasn't until later that we discovered the creature they're all descended from: *Indohyus*.[36] The earliest ancestors of the whale started as fish in the water, their later ancestors lived on the land (where they had legs), but after that the whales returned to the water. You discover the strangest things when you study evolution.

How Is a Butterfly Just like a Bird?

In Africa and South America, you find frogs that look exactly the same. They have the same shape, the same bright colors, and even the same markings. If you didn't know better, you'd think they were directly related. In actual fact, the ancestors of these frogs looked completely different. The little creatures only developed their colorful appearance later in their evolution.[37] One species of frog in Africa and the other in South America. It sounds like a really bizarre coincidence, but there's logic to it. The color has a particular function: to warn other animals about the frogs' poison. The most poisonous frogs and insects can be recognized by their bright colors.

Evolution doesn't necessarily mean that animals keep on becoming more and more different. Sometimes they evolve into the most convenient form and the most useful colors. Then they start to resemble one another more closely. This happens with butterflies. Some species aren't related, but it's almost impossible to tell them apart. There's even a moth that looks just like a bird: the hummingbird hawk-moth. The moth and the bird drink nectar from flowers with long petals. They both need a long beak or tongue. And they both have to hover in front of the flower. So, in large part, they need similar body structure.[38] Around coral reefs there are fish known as cleaner fish, which are little fish that clean big fish such as sharks; they remove all of the parasites from the sharks' skin like a beautician and then eat up all the pieces of meat left between the shark's teeth like a dental hygienist. All of these cleaner fish are very similar to one another—and to the cleaner shrimp, which provides exactly the same service but isn't a fish.[39] Wood lice and millipedes are also very alike. But are they family? Nope.

Can Mantises Play the Violin?

Sometimes animals start to resemble one another because their form is so useful for survival. But sometimes one animal will resemble another animal in order to fool yet other creatures; this is called mimicry. Other groups of frogs with equally colorful markings can live near the colored poison frogs. They pretend to be the same kind of dangerous poison frogs. In fact, they're not poisonous at all.[40] Fake cleaner fish, like the bluestriped fangblennies, are practically identical to real cleaner fishes and live in the same neighborhood. That means the big fish don't mind when these little creatures come closer. But while the big fish are hoping for a beauty treatment, the fake cleaner fish suddenly take a bite of the large beast. And then they quickly make themselves scarce.[41]

Pretending to be something different can be very handy, especially if you don't want to get eaten. You've probably seen a moth that looks a lot like a leaf. Now that's clever, because moth eaters don't like to eat leaves. As long as its enemies think it's a leaf, the moth is safe. Mantises are champions at imitating other animals and things. Some insects in the family look just like leaves. Others are impossible to distinguish from twigs. There are some that can perfectly imitate a piece of tree bark. And then there are those that can do a fantastic impersonation of an orchid.[42] Others have disguised themselves as dead wood, ants, snakes, or grass. There's even a mantis that looks like a violin. But that's just a coincidence.[43]

SO WHAT HAPPENED TO THE FISH IN US?

Evolution is a tricky subject. For every rule connected to evolution, you can come up with an exception, and there are even exceptions to that! It's hardly surprising that lots of people make errors of reasoning when they're talking

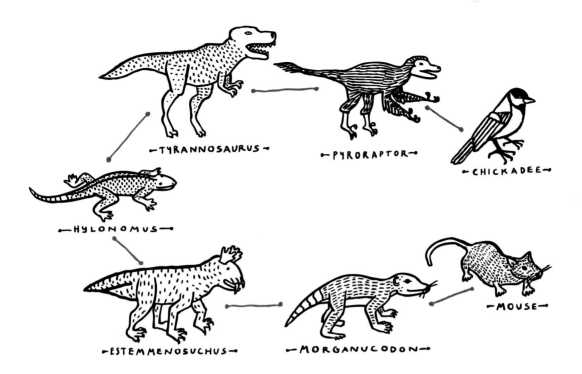

about evolution. One of the most common mistakes is the idea that we're descended from chimpanzees. Another common error is: If we're descended from the apes, then why are there still apes? And there's yet another mistake that's often made: If we come from the same animals as the other mammals do, why has a fossil of a rabbit-human or a bear-human never been found?

We're not descended from the chimpanzee, but we do have the same ancestor as the chimpanzee. That ancestor didn't really look like humans and not much like chimpanzees. It was, quite simply, a different animal. Some of its descendants evolved into chimpanzees. Others went in an entirely different direction and became human beings. These descendants of our common ancestor branched off in different directions. The same happened with the ancestors of other mammals. There's a good reason why we arrange our ancestors in a "family tree." We come from the same branch as the chimpanzees. If you go back a few branches, we're on the same branch as rabbits and bears. But there's no direct branch between rabbit or bear and human. And that's why you'll never find a fossil of a rabbit-human or a bear-human.

Is the Chickadee a Distant Cousin of *Tyrannosaurus rex*?

If you go all the way back to *Tiktaalik*, you'll soon find a spot where the branches split. The amphibians evolved from *Tiktaalik*, and those species split after a few million years. One group remained amphibians. From this group came the salamanders and frogs that we still have today. The other group developed into reptiles. The oldest reptile ever found is *Hylonomus*, a lizard-like creature.[44]

Soon after *Hylonomus*, that branch splits again. One group continued in the direction of the reptiles. This group was hugely successful for about 160 million years. The vast majority of large land animals in that period were reptiles. It was the age of the dinosaurs—who were all reptiles! The creatures that evolved into the fearsome *Pyroraptor*, the colossal *Diplodocus*, and the terrifying *Tyrannosaurus* lived during this period but so did the lizard, the gecko, and the snake, which we still have today. A group of dinosaurs also evolved with hair that was kind of like dreadlocks. The hair slowly changed into feathers, and those animals evolved into birds.[45] That sweet little chickadee hopping around in your garden is actually a distant relation of *Tyrannosaurus rex*. Okay, make that a very, very, very distant relation.

But a Mammal Doesn't Lay Eggs, Does It?

The other branch that developed after *Hylonomus* grew in the direction of the mammal-like reptiles. Some reptiles developed increasingly mammalian characteristics. *Estemmenosuchus*, for example, had antlers, and its skin didn't have any scales, as a reptile's would.[46] Sometime after that, *Thrinaxodon* made its way through the jungle. That animal was one of the first to grow hair, chewed with the teeth of a mammal, and was probably warm-blooded.[47] Reptiles are cold-blooded. They need the warmth of the sun to get going. Mammals generate their own heat within their bodies and often have fur to keep them warm. Scientists always assumed that dinosaurs were cold-blooded. They were reptiles, after all. But in recent years, dinosaurs have also been found with a downy coat.[48] It's possible that warm-blooded dinosaurs also existed.

Later still, we meet *Morganucodon* in the jungle. This creature was quite a lot like a mouse, with its whiskers and short hair. It was probably warm-blooded, but it still laid eggs, like a reptile.[49] Mammal mothers don't lay eggs. They give birth to ready-made babies. Well, they usually do. But there are, of course, exceptions. The echidna is one such eggy exception. As is the duckbilled platypus. All of the mammal-like reptiles are extinct now, but reptile-like mammals, like the echidna and the duckbilled platypus, are still around.[50]

WHAT MADE THE DINOSAURS EXTINCT?

Some steps of evolution seem almost impossible. Like the step from non-living to living. Or the step from sea creature to land creature. But there always turns out to be some kind of intermediate form that provides the solution. The move from laying eggs to giving birth seems like another unbridgeable gap. And yet there's an in-between form there too. The shift from egg to womb goes via the pouch. The ancestors of the kangaroos provide the answer to the question of how mammals managed to make the move from hatching eggs.

Why Don't People Come from Eggs?

The mother's pouch takes over the role of the protective eggshell. Marsupials, as we call animals that grow inside a pouch, are born very early, when they're the size of a small shrimp. Once they're inside the pouch, they continue to grow and develop. And when they're ready, they can finally leave the front pocket in their mother's fur. Until then, it's nice and safe and warm inside the pouch. The mother doesn't have to sit and wait for an egg to hatch, which is a lot more convenient than all the hard work that birds and reptiles have to do. Male penguins, for example, stand over their eggs constantly during the coldest months of the year in the coldest place on Earth. The lucky marsupials don't have to do that.

Mammals actually have all kinds of advantages over reptiles and birds. They don't have to sit on eggs, which means they're safer because they can leave when they want to without worrying about their eggs getting cold. They're not dependent on warmth from the sun, so they can also go hunting for food at night and live in cooler regions. And they can grow bigger brains. Brains need a huge amount of energy to grow. And that requires a huge amount of nourishment. Even the largest egg we know, the ostrich egg, contains only 2,000 calories.[51] That's all the calories that are available to help the ostrich chick grow. But a human mother can feed that amount of calories to her baby in less than a week. A newborn ostrich has a brain that's only the size of a walnut, while a human baby has a gigantic brain in comparison to other animals.

FAMOUS MARSUPIALS

KANGAROO (*Macropodidae*) ▲▮▼▮▼ KOALA (*Phascolarctos cinereus*) ▮▲▮

How Deadly Can a Meteorite Be?

But all those big-brained human babies might never have existed if the Earth hadn't been struck by a major disaster. The reptiles still reigned supreme until that time. There was no room at all for large mammals; mouse-like creatures were safe to venture out only at night. By day, the mosasaurs, fearsome lizard-looking snakes, ruled the waters.[52] The pterosaurs ruled the sky, and they were no angels either. And the land was ruled by those terrifying dinosaurs with their gigantic proportions. It was the age of the giants. But that all changed when something terrible happened.[53] Around 65 million years ago something happened that killed off every land animal heavier than about 55 pounds.

Most scientists believe this disaster was a huge meteorite impact. Evidence of just such an immense impact has been found on the Yucatan

Peninsula in Mexico. It sounds strange that just one meteorite could wipe out so many animals. But it wasn't just any old impact. If you were there (and you wouldn't have wanted to be) you would have seen this: a meteor strike with the explosive power of thousands and thousands of nuclear bombs exploding at the same place at once. All that energy caused a blast wave of fire like you have only seen in science-fiction movies: a ring of fire expanding for thousands of miles. In the meantime a huge shockwave made the Earth tremble, setting off landslides, tsunamis, and volcanic eruptions around the world. The heat of the impact caused forest fires that were so widespread they filled the sky of the entire planet with soot. The sunlight could no longer reach the Earth, which subsequently cooled down. I told you you wouldn't want to have been there . . . [54]

Another explanation for the end of the dinosaurs is that there were a vast number of serious volcanic eruptions that occurred during the end of the Cretaceous period. There were huge explosions that spewed an inconceivable amount of ash into the air. Some people believe these eruptions alone were severe enough to make the dinosaurs extinct.

The Rise of the Mammals?

Whatever happened, the era of the dinosaurs ended with a bang around 65 million years ago. After that, the Earth recovered. Slowly but surely, life on the land scrambled to its feet. But an end had come to the reign of the reptiles. Only the smallest reptiles had survived the disaster. The age of the mammals was dawning. At first there were just small rodents. But before long they evolved into tigers, elephants, whales, deer, and apes with their big brains. That's just as well, because with a reptile brain you'd never have been smart enough to learn how to read this book.

Has the Story of Evolution Been Proven for Sure?

EVOLUTION—GOOD SENSE OR NONSENSE?

In the United States, 47 percent of the people believe that evolution is real.[1] In Sweden, Germany, China, and Japan, the figures are higher: 68, 65, 64, and 60 percent, respectively. In Indonesia, 57 percent of the people believe in creationism, not evolution, and in South Africa, 56 percent. In Turkey, 60 percent of the people believe in creationism, and in Saudi Arabia it's 75 percent.[2] So many people in the world believe in creationism and not evolution. Can we be sure evolution is true?

It's not so surprising that so many people don't believe in evolution. At many schools, it's normal that the Bible story be taught in class as the only explanation for life on Earth.[3] If you've never heard another explanation, you just keep on believing that story. You have to know about the theory of evolution before you can believe in it. And the more you know, the more likely you are to believe in it.

Does Every Scientist Believe in Evolution?

There are hardly any scientists nowadays who believe that the Earth is at most only 10,000 years old. If you think the Earth and the universe are that young, then you're doubting most of the physicists, chemists, biologists, astronomers, geologists, and even mathematicians. Not all of them? No. There are a few exceptions: scientists who have come up with theories to explain how creation could have taken place in six days after all. But their fellow scientists don't take them too seriously. There's such a vast amount of evidence for the Earth being billions of years old.

People who believe that God made the Earth are called creationists. There are two ways of being a creationist. You can believe that God made the Earth but that he did it over the course of billions of years in an evolution-like way.

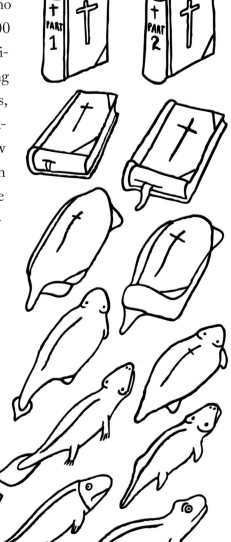

CHAPTER 10: HAS THE STORY OF EVOLUTION BEEN PROVEN FOR SURE?

159

Really, you believe in both God *and* evolution. There are many people who think this way, including lots of scientists. But when I mention creationists in this book from now on, I'm talking about people who deny that evolution has ever taken place. The strict believers. The people who believe that everything in the Bible truly happened. Absolutely everything.

The Bible says nothing about evolution, fossils, and the development of new species. For this reason, creationists say the theory of evolution can't be true. They have lots and lots of arguments in favor of the Biblical version of creation. They ask intelligent questions that are enough to make you start to doubt.

"THE THEORY OF EVOLUTION IS A THEORY. SO EVOLUTION HAS NOT BEEN PROVEN."

Lots of creationists say that evolution is "just a theory," so there is no evidence. Well, they don't know the exact meaning of the term *scientific theory*. A theory is a scientific explanation. You have a question that you want to investigate, and you try to find an answer by thinking carefully about it, and testing your ideas. When you've gathered proof for your ideas, you call it a theory.[4] Darwin wondered how life on the land had begun. By reasoning logically, he realized that the transition from fish to reptiles must have happened via amphibians. He also collected an enormous amount of proof. He really could call his idea a theory.

Which Animal on Earth will Survive for Longest?

Another way to prove ideas is by experimenting. In those cases you search for a scientific explanation by testing ideas or doing experiments to answer your questions. For example: are there any multicellular creatures that can

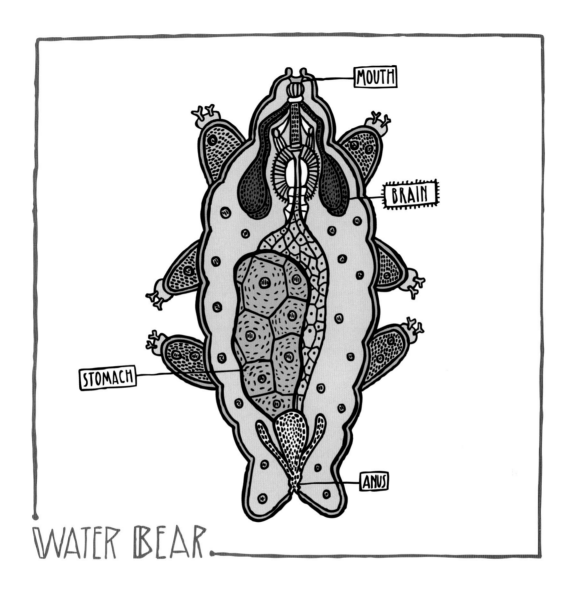

MOUTH

BRAIN

STOMACH

ANUS

WATER BEAR

survive temperatures of both -400 degrees Fahrenheit and 300 degrees Fahrenheit? You don't need to be a professor to work out how to investigate this question. Find animals, put them in an oven, then throw them in the freezer, and then see if they're still alive. There's no need to try it out with

CHAPTER 10: HAS THE STORY OF EVOLUTION BEEN PROVEN FOR SURE?

161

5

ducks, frogs, or Joe Schmo from Buffalo, of course. They're sure to die. But it's a different story with water bears.

Water bears, better known as tardigrades, are tiny little animals that grow no longer than six one-hundredths of an inch.[6] They're found all over the planet: in springs of boiling water, but also on the summits of the Himalayas, where it's sometimes -75 degrees. It's a perfect animal for testing purposes. Heat up a tardigrade to 300 degrees and then cool it down to -400 degrees and see if it's still alive. What happens? The tardigrade wakes up after all this torture, has a little yawn, and then goes about its tardigrade business as if nothing had happened.[7]

Well, okay, I made up the bit about the yawning. But the rest of it's true. If the Earth ever becomes an inhospitable planet with huge swings in temperature, then the tardigrade will probably just keep on living.

Why Do Some People Believe *Tiktaalik* Is Not Proof of Evolution?

How does the theory of evolution work in practice? Well, in practice, huge numbers of fossils have been found that show how new species have come about through evolution. Just take a look at *Thrinaxodon* and *Morganucodon*, which lived between reptiles and mammals. Or *Tiktaalik*, which was somewhere between fish and amphibians.

But for the strict creationists, those fossils aren't proof of evolution. While *Tiktaalik* has been found, we're still missing the link between *Tiktaalik* and *Acanthostega*. And if such a "Tiktaalostega" is ever found, the creationists probably still won't be satisfied. They're sure to demand to see the transition from "Tiktaalostega" to *Acanthostega*. The creationists also think that the fossils are too different from one another. According to them, the sizes of these missing links are too big or too small, the number of bones is not the same, or there is another great difference, so there can be no connection between them.[8]

Do Werewolves and Ostrich People Exist?

Funnily enough, there are also human beings of different sizes and with nonstandard toes. Many members of the Vadoma tribe in Africa have only two toes on each foot. This is the result of a small mutation in their genes. They find their "ostrich feet" very useful. They come in handy when they're climbing trees.[9] In Ecuador there are people with a different kind of genetic abnormality. They remain very small. They have largely the same physique as other people, but they only come up to most people's waists. They're happy with their bodies, too. They don't suffer from two serious conditions that affect many other people: cancer and diabetes.[10]

In Mexico, there are people who seem a lot like werewolves. They have hair all over their bodies, including their faces. Again, this is because of

CHAPTER 10: HAS THE STORY OF EVOLUTION BEEN PROVEN FOR SURE?

163

their genes.[11] There are other people on the planet with the same condition. Nature sometimes makes mistakes. Sometimes these "mistakes" actually turn out to be useful, and that's how differences between people come about.

Are You Descended from Genghis Khan?

If Genghis Khan had been a member of the Vadoma tribe, then perhaps we wouldn't think having two toes on each foot was unusual. Genghis

Khan was an important chieftain who founded the Mongol empire 800 years ago. He is said to have killed millions of people as he conquered. He also fathered children with countless numbers of women.[12] Scientists have used DNA to prove that no fewer than 8 percent of all men in Asia (that's half a percent of all men on Earth) are direct descendants of this infamous Mongolian.[13]

But Genghis Khan was not a Vadoma. And the Vadoma are not a warlike people who go off looting and making babies everywhere. What we think of as normal depends on chance and past events. The number of toes, the size

CHAPTER 10: HAS THE STORY OF EVOLUTION BEEN PROVEN FOR SURE?

165

of our bodies: these are things that can vary, even within the same species. And often there are no intermediate forms; there is no group of three- or four-toed people between the Vadoma and people with five toes, for instance. But fossils and intermediate forms don't have to be the only proof of evolution. Because there's another way to prove evolution in practice.

How Can You See Evolution for Yourself?

You can see evolution at work every day, just by keeping your eyes open. By noticing that the moths in London were a much darker color when it was a dirty city with lots of soot. By seeing that nature is constantly in motion and that new species are always coming and going as environments change. Or by talking to fishermen. Because they'll tell you that the cod they fish for are getting smaller and smaller.

The fish are getting smaller because the fishermen are not

permitted to catch small cod. The rules say a cod has to be a certain length before you're allowed to catch it. If it's any shorter, it gets thrown back into the sea. If you're a fish, it's worth staying small. And the results are clear. In recent years, cod have become much smaller. They mature earlier and start reproducing at a younger age.[14] There are hundreds of similar examples of evolution, right under our noses.

Can a Species of Lizard Change in Just 36 Years?

You can put evolution to the test. This is exactly what biologist Anthony Herrel did. He put five pairs of lizards on an island that was not previously inhabited by their species. Then he didn't return for 36 years.[15] He found the descendants of the five pairs of lizards. He could tell they were the right ones by looking at their DNA. He compared the lizards to the species they came from and discovered that the island lizards had changed considerably after all that time. For example, they had much larger heads and their bite was much stronger. And unlike the other members of their species, they mainly ate plants instead of insects. It was clearly easier to find plants on the island. The lizards that had stayed on the mainland had of course remained exactly the same. They had no reason to change.

Thirty-six years is a rather long time to wait for an experiment. It can go

CHAPTER 10: HAS THE STORY OF EVOLUTION BEEN PROVEN FOR SURE?

167

faster than that. But you'll have to use species that reproduce much more quickly, such as bacteria. They can do it in just a few hours or even minutes. That's why biologists like experimenting on these little creatures. *Escherichia coli* is a particularly popular test subject. It's one of the most common bacteria on the planet. There are around a hundred billion billion of them on Earth.[16] You've got plenty of them sitting in your gut right now. So, yes, they're very suitable bacteria for experiments.

What Kind of Dull Experiment Took 20 Years?

The experiment went as follows: scientists put the *E. coli* bacteria in dishes and then added glucose and citrate. Glucose is a kind of sugar, and citrate is an inedible substance. Then they watched to see what would happen. If you were to do the experiment yourself, you'd see that at first the number of bacteria increases rapidly and then that this process stops at a certain point. That makes sense. The glucose is eventually used up, and there's nothing left to eat. The population can't grow.

That's what the researchers expected to happen. But they took their job seriously and didn't use just 1 dish but 12. And they kept them completely separate. Every day, they removed exactly 1 percent of the volume of the bacteria from one dish and started a new colony in a different dish. For all of the 12 "tribes." And they did the same again and again. Day after day. Week after week. Year after year. Throughout the experiment, they regularly compared the bacteria and the size of the colonies in each of the dishes.

And Was the Experiment Worth All That Effort?

It sounds like an incredibly dull experiment. Boring bacteria, in boring dishes, with boring food. For 20 long years. But it gave the researchers

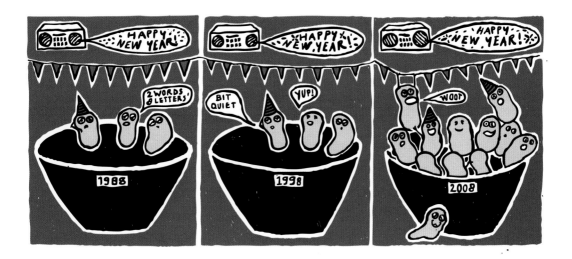

the perfect opportunity to study the differences between the modern bacteria, their parents, their grandparents, their great-grandparents, their great-great-grandparents, their great-great-great-grandparents, and so on, and so on (all the way through 45,000 *greats*). This took 20 years. If you compare that to humans, you get to ancestors from 1 million years ago.

And yes, the experiment was worth the effort. Because something really did change. Slowly but surely, the number of bacteria in each dish started to increase by the end of the day. But not at the same speed in every dish. The bacteria in some dishes were becoming better and better at surviving and reproducing in a dish of glucose than others. In 10,000 generations, some of the bacteria grew twice as fast as in other dishes. That was pretty much what the researchers had anticipated. But after around 33,000 great-grandchildren, something spectacular happened in one of the dishes. Something that instantly made up for all those years of boredom. From then on, the number of bacteria grew enormously! The colonies became six times larger. Not slowly, either, but almost overnight.[17]

CHAPTER 10: HAS THE STORY OF EVOLUTION BEEN PROVEN FOR SURE?

169

What Do These Bacteria Mean for the Theory of Evolution?

What was going on? How could the colonies of bacteria grow so spectacularly in such a short time? Some of the bacteria had succeeded in using the citrate, that inedible substance, as a food source. That meant there was suddenly way more food in their dish. Very soon, the bacteria had developed into a completely different species, which was much better at surviving in those conditions.[18] A kind that had a completely different diet. It's as if you could suddenly start eating sand and stones when you feel hungry. That's not evolutionary—it's revolutionary! This study represented a huge breakthrough in our thinking about evolution. Evolution can proceed very slowly and evenly, but it can also make huge jumps and move at lightning speed.

Back to the theory of evolution. Darwin explained, through careful observation and logical thinking, how different species can develop. That is the theory. Reality proves that evolution takes place right under our noses. That is the practice. Darwin's theory is still called a theory, even though it's been proven in all kinds of different ways. A scientific theory isn't an "unproven idea." A theory can be a recognized fact.

"NATURE WORKS PERFECTLY. IT'S SO WONDERFUL THAT IT MUST HAVE BEEN DESIGNED BY A GOD."

As I mentioned back near the beginning of the book, many people through-out the ages have come to the conclusion that nature must have been designed by a god. Just listen to the birds in May. Or look at the setting sun above the snowy mountaintops or the colors of the corals or the clever way some

animals are made. How can all of those magnificent things have developed through the process of evolution? But there's another side to nature. A dark and ugly one. The side of creatures like the liver fluke.

Who Would Make a Sheep Die a Slow and Painful Death?

Sometimes you spot an ant sitting on the tip of a blade of grass in a field. What's it doing? Enjoying the view? No. The ant has no business being there. There's no food up there, and it's a very dangerous place to be. It could be eaten by a sheep at any moment. And that's exactly the intention. Not the ant's

CHAPTER 10: HAS THE STORY OF EVOLUTION BEEN PROVEN FOR SURE?

171

intention, of course, but the intention of a miserable little wormy creature: the liver fluke. The fluke is so small that it can take up residence in the ant's brain. And then it takes control of the ant's thinking processes. It crawls inside the ant's brain and changes the poor insect's behavior so that it suddenly attaches itself to that blade of grass. Which is exactly what the liver fluke wants.

Liver flukes have a purpose. They have to find their way into a sheep's intestines, where they can reproduce. And to make that journey from the ground into the sheep's gut, they turn the ant into a kind of zombie. The zombie ant gets eaten by the sheep. The liver flukes pass through the stomach into the animal's liver, and from there, they hop into the blood. A few weeks later, they end up in the gut, where they lay their eggs. The larvae that are produced can eat all the lovely sheep poop they want, their favorite food. The liver fluke's long journey was a success!

That's all very nice for the liver fluke, of course, but it's really bad news for the ant. Because the ant dies. And it's lousy for the sheep too. Having liver flukes in their systems can make sheep sick and even cause them to die a nasty, painful death. It's not just sheep that are killed by liver flukes but also horses, cows, and other grazing animals.[19]

Yay for Nature?

That's just one species of liver fluke. There are other kinds too, ones that pick on birds, for instance. All kinds of beautiful animals have to die so that the offspring of a bunch of insignificant, puny, rotten poop-eating worms can live. Yay for nature? Hmm, no, not really. Nature also means that sheep and baby polar bears and seals have to die. That sickness and hunger exist. Or that a pesky mosquito can keep you awake all night. Grr!

If there's one place you can expect to find murder, looting, and cruelty, it's in nature. Animals can't live forever. That's easy enough to grasp. Eventually they have to die. But why does it have to happen in such a nasty, painful way? Nature isn't all that wonderful, after all. And our own design isn't quite as clever as you might think, either. Have you ever suffered from hiccups? You're not the only one. Lots and lots of mammals have had a bellyful of hiccups. Charles Osborne of Iowa in particular: he had hiccups for 68 years, and they only stopped a year before his death.[20] A pope, Pius XII, actually died while having hiccups for months in a row, though it wasn't the hiccups that killed him.[21] So what is the point of this bizarre condition? Well, there is no point to hiccups. But we know exactly why we get them—it's because our ancestors were fish.

Why Do Sharks Never Get Hiccups, but We Do?

There are some things we don't need to think about. Breathing is automatic, for example. And that's just as well. Imagine you were doing a difficult test and you had to keep thinking, *Breathe in, breathe out*, so you wouldn't die. Breathing comes automatically to fish too. A certain part of their brains takes care of the process, so that they can pay attention to more important things. Lungfish and amphibians don't have to make any effort to breathe. But breathing's a bit more dangerous for them. They have to get oxygen into their lungs, but not water. For that reason, they have a nerve that makes their windpipe close whenever they're at risk of water getting into their lungs. We've inherited this nerve from the amphibians, even though we don't spend that much time in the water these days.

In humans, that nerve runs all the way from our brains to our diaphragms. And as soon as the nerve is stimulated, it closes off our throat just for a moment. That's the same reaction that amphibians have to make sure water doesn't get into their lungs. But it gives humans the hiccups. That first hiccup is usually followed by a few more. If you can stop within five

CHAPTER 10: HAS THE STORY OF EVOLUTION BEEN PROVEN FOR SURE?

173

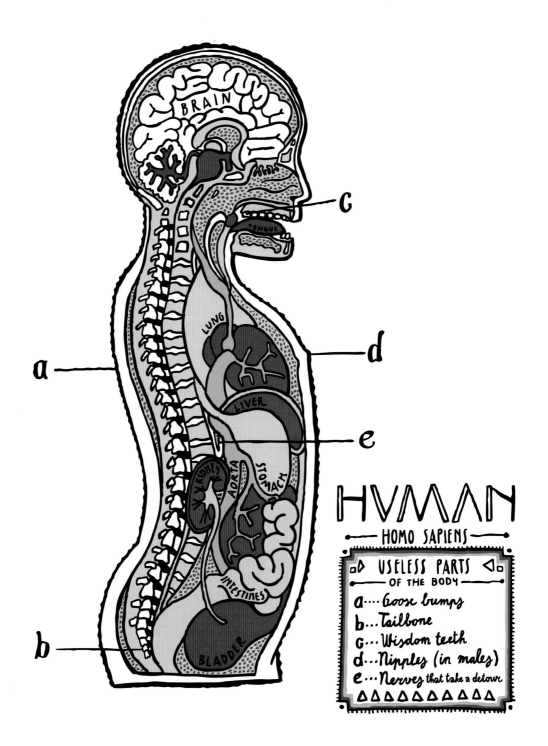

HVMAN
HOMO SAPIENS

USELESS PARTS
OF THE BODY
a.... Goose bumps
b... Tailbone
c... Wisdom teeth
d... Nipples (in males)
e... Nerves that take a detour

hiccups, you're lucky. Because if you don't, a kind of mechanism kicks off in our body that keeps the hiccups going. That's why hiccups can sometimes last so long. The problem is that our water-valve nerve often gets stimulated because it's so long.[22] A clever designer would run a very short nerve from our diaphragm to our throat. Then it wouldn't get bothered so frequently. In fish, the nerve goes from their brains to their gills. That's only a very short distance. And that's why sharks never get hiccups.

Why Do We Have the Nerves of a Fish?

Our nerves are the perfect proof that we have fish as ancestors. In fish, the nerves work in a very logical way, taking the shortest route from one part of the body to another. But our ancestors gradually evolved from fish until they developed our physique. And as part of the process, our nerves took an increasingly long and complicated route. You have one nerve that goes from your brain to the larynx, or voice box, in your throat. If you measured the distance with a ruler, it's about four inches, but the nerve's way longer than that. It heads straight for your chest and then takes a few weird detours before finally going to the throat. And don't think we humans have the weirdest design of all. Giraffes have much longer necks. In a giraffe, the same nerve goes all the way down and back up the entire neck, covering a distance of about 16 feet, even though the spot it needs to reach is only a few inches away.[23]

An airplane builder can decide from one day to the next to replace a propeller with a jet engine. But evolution doesn't work that easily. If you want to turn a propeller into a jet plane and every version in between has to be able to fly (because, of course, every intermediate form in evolution has to be able to live), then you end up with a bizarre kind of jet engine. And I'm sorry to say this, but you and I are at least as strangely put together as that bizarre jet engine.

CHAPTER 10: HAS THE STORY OF EVOLUTION BEEN PROVEN FOR SURE?

175

Why Do We Get Goose Bumps?

There are plenty of crazy things in nature. Cave salamanders have eyes, even though they live in pitch darkness and never see daylight. Why do they have eyes? Eyes are just a nuisance for them. Like it costs energy and effort for a bodybuilder to create muscles, it also costs energy for every growing creature to grow eyes. Eyes make you vulnerable because they are weak and unprotected and make it possible for germs to enter the body.[24] But still cave salamanders have eyes. That's because they're descended from salamanders that lived in the light.

We get goose bumps when we're cold. There's no point to them. Why do they happen? Because we're descended from animals with fur. And animals with fur become warmer when their hair stands on end. Anyone who's ever bumped their tailbone will have wondered what that useless thing is actually for. As the name suggests, we have a tailbone because our ancestors had tails. That little bone, also known as the coccyx, is all that remains of that tail.

You could fill a book with examples of nature's useless body parts. A very thick book indeed!

"BUT WHAT ABOUT THE BOMBARDIER BEETLE? OR THE EYE?"

As you'll have realized, my belief in evolution is rock solid. I don't doubt it at all. I haven't doubted it for years. But when I first heard about the bombardier beetle, I did briefly wonder if I'd gotten my wires crossed. Creationists often use this beetle to prove Darwin got it wrong. But Darwin had his own battle with that beetle.

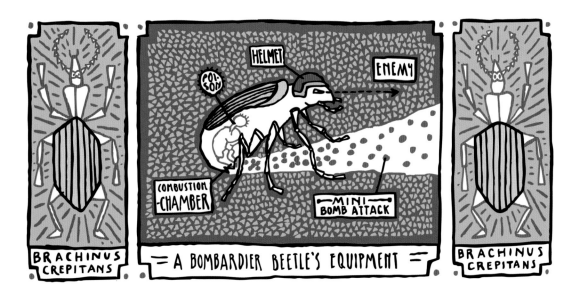

BRACHINUS CREPITANS

= A BOMBARDIER BEETLE'S EQUIPMENT =

BRACHINUS CREPITANS

There's a Beetle with Its Own Air-Defense System?

Darwin collected all kinds of things, but he was proudest of his beetle collection. As soon as he got to a new place, he went out looking for beetles, which he took home with him. In his diary, he wrote that he once saw a magnificent specimen of a beetle that he'd never encountered before. It would be a great addition to his collection. He picked up the beetle and walked on, pleased with his find. Lo and behold, a few feet farther on, there was another remarkable new beetle. That one went in his other hand. Believe it or not, he walked on a short way and spotted a third new beetle! He already had two in his hands, and he didn't want to miss out on the third. He couldn't put a specimen in his pocket because it might die. So he popped one of the beetles into his mouth!

As soon as Darwin put the beetle into his mouth, it felt as if the creature exploded. Darwin's mouth started to burn, and there was a terrible taste. Darwin quickly spat it out.[25] It turned out that it must have been

CHAPTER 10: HAS THE STORY OF EVOLUTION BEEN PROVEN FOR SURE?

177

a bombardier beetle. The bombardier beetle is a beetle with two chemical substances in its back. When everything's nice and quiet, the two substances remain neatly separated. But when the beetle's in danger, it aims its tail at its enemy. It mixes up the chemicals, and then there appears to be a big explosion. The beetle squirts a liquid that's close to the boiling point of water, 212 degrees, into its attacker's eyes, blinding it for a moment. In the meantime, the bombardier beetle makes a quick escape.[26]

What's the Bombardier Beetle's Secret?

So you and I may be like a bizarre jet engine, but the bombardier beetle is a fine example of perfection. Imagine that the little beetle had been just a bit different, that one of the substances had a slightly different composition. Then there wouldn't have been an explosion. Or the explosion could have been even bigger and blown the beetle to bits. Or what if the substances had combined too soon? Or too late? No, the beetle's settings are just right. If you started tinkering with the bombardier beetle, it wouldn't work as well. But evolution means the creature must have been different at some point. Where does the bombardier beetle come from? 1–0 to the creationists, you could say.

It would make a nice conundrum for a riddle book. But you don't actually have enough information to find the answer. What you need to know is that there are huge numbers of beetles. We don't even know exactly how many. There are at least 300,000 species of beetles, maybe even as many as 500,000.[27] And what you also need to know is that the two substances that the bombardier beetle has on its back aren't even that unusual. They're in the pigments that give the beetle its camouflage coloring. In addition to being so hot, the substances taste absolutely disgusting, so there are hardly any animals that would ever want to eat such a gross beetle.

Why Is the Bombardier Beetle Actually Proof of Evolution?

If you play a video clip of the bombardier beetle in slow motion, you'll see that there's no explosion inside the beetle's body. The beetle actually ejects the substances in a series of dozens of mini bombardments. The substances don't combine and start to burn until they're outside the body. But the most important fact is that there are other kinds of beetles that are nowhere near as good at making bombs. Instead of a well-aimed blast, what comes out of their bodies is just a bit of foamy gunk. But that's enough to make a spider or a bird make a face and give the beetle a wide berth.[28] Also, a bomb-making machine is very handy, but it's not essential to a beetle's survival. Those hundreds of thousands of other species can't throw bombs, but they're not extinct yet. So there could have been plenty of intermediate forms that eventually led to the spectacular bombardier beetle. And the scientists score the equalizer: 1–1.

The funniest thing of all is that, according to science, the bombardier beetle is actually one of the proofs that the creationists' story is incorrect. Because the Bible says that, in the beginning, Earth was a paradise. There were no predators feeding on the other animals, and everyone was happy. But one day the first people on Earth, Adam and Eve, picked an apple from a tree, even though God had said it was forbidden. That caused all kinds of trouble. God became angry and punished every living creature on Earth for this crime. Paradise was over. Humans and animals suffered pain and death, and from then on animals ate other animals.

And that's the story the creationists believe.

Why Would Anyone Need Weapons in a Paradise?

But then . . . why did God equip the bombardier beetle with this weapon? There were no predators in paradise. So why would a beetle need an

CHAPTER 10: HAS THE STORY OF EVOLUTION BEEN PROVEN FOR SURE?

179

air-defense system? You don't need defenses if you're not going to get eaten, do you? The story in the Bible can't be true. Final score: science wins 2–1.

WHAT'S WRONG WITH YOUR EYES?

Have you ever stopped to think about the fact that human beings can see? That something can happen somewhere many miles away and that we receive those images inside our head at a staggering speed? And in color too! There's an amazing device that allows us to do this: the eye. And we have not just one of them but two. That means we can judge distances.

What's So Great about Our Eyes?

The human eye is a wonder of technology. One of the most important parts of the eye is called the retina. This is a layer of light-sensitive cells that transmit information about the light along nerve cells to the brain. The eye sits safely inside the head, and all of the light comes in through the iris. The iris is just a hole that lets the light in. But there's another important part: the lens. This lens allows us to see clearly when things are in the distance and also when they're close up. The perfect combination of iris, lens, and retina

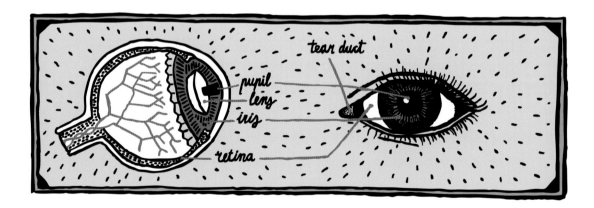

means we don't have to make any effort to see in sharp focus. The eye auto-matically adapts. Tear ducts beside the eye keep it nice and clean. Our eye-lids work like windshield wipers. Great, huh? It works perfectly, doesn't it?

Where Did Our Eyes Come From?

How do you get from nothing (the first animals were completely blind) to such a fantastically functioning eye? Well, it was actually pretty simple. We can see from existing species how the evolution of the eye worked, from old animals to new ones. Some jellyfish have just a few light-sensitive cells. All they can do is perceive light. But that's all they need. It's certainly good enough for them to have survived as a species for hundreds of millions of years. Flatworms, also one of the first species on Earth, have eyes. But theirs consist of nothing more than flat retinas. Flatworm eyes have no lenses and no irises, which means they cannot focus. They are not capable of perceiving shapes, but they can make out light and movement. That's enough for the flatworm to tell if an enemy is approaching. And that's all it needs to know. Flatworms don't read the newspaper anyway.

There are also animals, like the nautilus, that have retinas and irises. This creature has a spherical eye, like humans do. The nautilus can see shapes, light, and movement. But its eye doesn't have a lens. If the animal wanted to focus, it would need to wear glasses. Anyway, the next step leads to the kind of eyes that we have: with a retina, iris, and lens. It's that simple. So simple, in fact, that the eye has developed a number of times, in different ways. Insects, for example, have a very different kind of eye. They see through hundreds of tiny eyes with lenses, all at the same time. That works perfectly too. They wouldn't want to swap with us. There are different types of eyes, all of which work excellently. The ability to see is very special, but it's also the most natural thing in the world.

CHAPTER 10: HAS THE STORY OF EVOLUTION BEEN PROVEN FOR SURE?

181

How Would You Design an Eye?

But that's not the whole story about our eyes. Imagine you had to design a digital camera. A camera with a retina at the back, a lens, and an iris. But also with wires to connect it to a computer and a printer. Where would you put those wires? Between the retina and the iris, where they would get in the way? Or on the outside, so that you would see a perfect image? Probably that one, eh? That's how anyone with any sense would do it. But our eyes don't work that way. What we see is disrupted by a tangle of tiny blood vessels and nerves in our eyes. There's no designer in the world who would construct an eye like that. Anyone who came up with such a dumb design would be instantly fired.

We even have a blind spot, where we can't see anything at all. That's the place on our retina where the nerves go to the brain. The blind spot is in a really awkward position. Try this little experiment: look at the circle below. Hold your head close to the paper, close your left eye, and stare at the circle with your right eye, then slowly move your head away from the paper. You'll notice that the plus sign disappears at a certain point.

The plus sign disappears because of the blind spot. If the nerves were connected to our retina in a different place, we wouldn't have this problem.

Aren't We Allowed to See Clearly?

We've established that our eye has a pretty weird design. But we still see clearly, don't we? That's right. But we could have seen much better if our eyes were smarter. It's a bit like looking outside through a net. It's only when you take down the net that you realize how much more you could have seen. Based on the theory of evolution, we can explain exactly how our eye came about and why its structure is so strange. If God deliberately designed our eye in this way, he can't have wanted us to see too well.

The eye and the bombardier beetle are just two examples that appear at first to be so ingenious that they must have been designed by a god but which ultimately provide evidence for evolution. There are plenty of other examples. If you still doubt evolution, you might as well just skip the rest of this book. Although . . . the rest of the book contains even more evidence for evolution. And it considers another question that we haven't answered yet: Where do human beings come from? How did we develop from those first mouse-like mammals into an intelligent life-form that can build computers? Into a special species of animal that has used submarines and airplanes to investigate the entire planet and far beyond? Into a curious creature that can explore the universe with telescopes and spaceships? And into . . . Joe Schmo from Buffalo?

CHAPTER 10: HAS THE STORY OF EVOLUTION BEEN PROVEN FOR SURE?

183

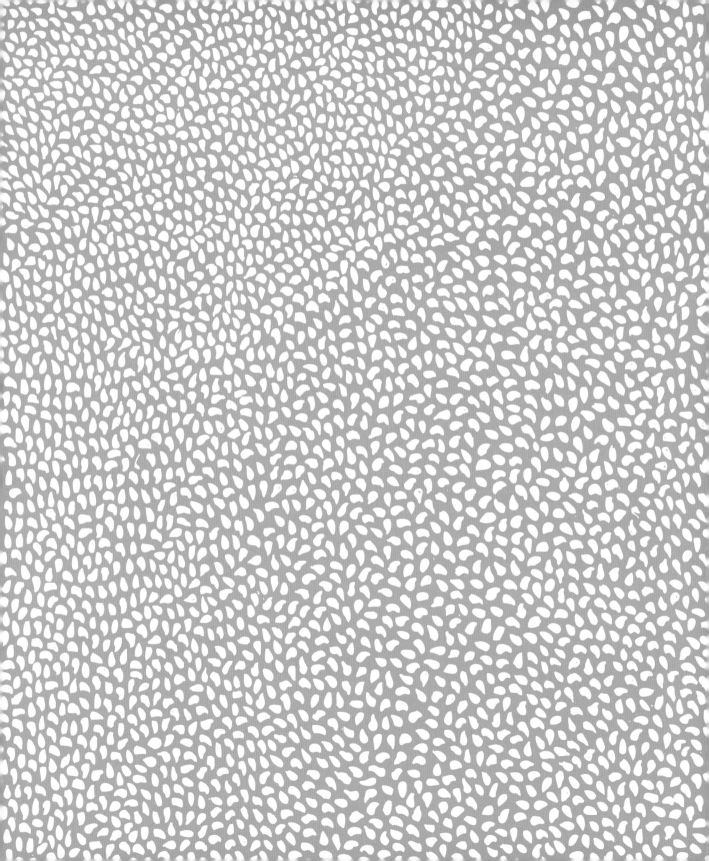

CHAPTER 11

From Mouse to Man

WHAT DID OUR ANCESTORS LOOK LIKE?

Here's a thought experiment: imagine Joe Schmo invents a rocket that will allow everyone to go into space. He opens a factory and starts building his Jo-schmo 1 rockets. It's a big success. His son Joe Schmo Jr. later takes over from his father and improves the rocket. He sells it as the Jo-schmo 2. Tony Schmo, Joe Jr.'s brother, starts his own rocket factory. He builds cargo rockets to transport things through space. He sells them under the name of To-schmo 1. Mo, Joe Jr. and Tony's sister, makes racing rockets. And she sells them as Mo-schmo 1.

Later, the children of Tony, Mo, and Joe Jr. start their own rocket factory. Some of them improve their parents' rockets. Others do things just a little bit differently. One of Tony's daughters builds extrabig cargo rockets, for instance, and her brother makes superfast cargo rockets. One of Mo's sons builds luxury racing rockets, and his sister makes racing rockets that are specially suitable for long distances. This goes on for hundreds of years. All of the children improve upon their parents' rockets or at least make a few tweaks. What you end up with is the To-schmo 27A Turbo Plus Deluxe: a cargo rocket that's superfast and ultramodern and perfectly suited for transporting small cargos over long distances.

Which Animal Are You Most Like?

What does that story have to do with evolution? Well, it *is* evolution. The children are all descended from the same ancestor, and their rockets are all just a little different. You could compare those rockets to our DNA. If you see a To-schmo rocket, you know that rocket was built by someone who had Tony Schmo as an ancestor. DNA works just the same. You can link certain pieces to a particular ancestor. As time goes by, the rockets will become less and less like the very first model. And the same applies to DNA. But we can see exactly who is descended from whom, and who's related to whom.

In the same way, we can look back at our own ancestors. Then we see that the most recent species, with which we share the most ancestors, are the chimpanzees and the bonobos. If you go back farther, we have the same ancestors as the gorillas. Then it's the orangutans. They're followed by the gibbons. These are all still apes. In more distant history, there are the monkeys and prosimians, such as ring-tailed lemurs. Eventually we come to very different mammals, like squirrel- and rodent-like creatures. And, of course, you can just keep on going.[1]

Why Do We Know So Little about Our Ancestors?

DNA shows us which animals we're most closely related to. But it doesn't tell us anything about what our ancestors once looked like. Those ancestors were not bonobos or gorillas but a completely different kind of ape, which became extinct long ago. If we want to see traces of our ancestors, we have to take a look at fossils. And those bones and teeth from the distant past can help us to find our way back into history.

You can find human bones in any graveyard. But there are also ones from way back into the past, until around 200,000 years ago.[2] From the time before that, you'll find only bones from humanlike creatures, a kind of

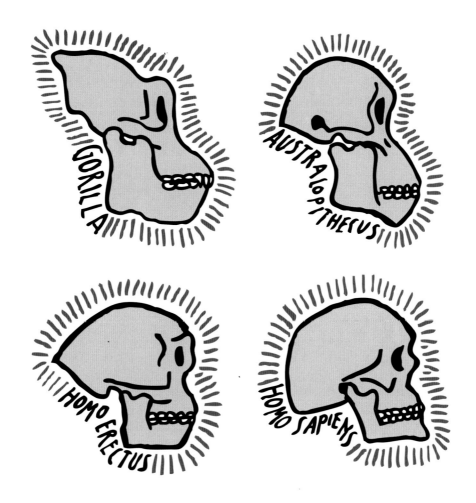

human-ape. If you go farther back, you won't find them anymore, but you'll find bones of ape species. The farther back in time you go, the smaller the apes and monkeys become. Until you only find bones of monkeys that most closely resembled a squirrel. And after that you come to the small mouse-like mammals that lived back in the time of the dinosaurs.

That all sounds logical and well organized, but in reality it's chaos. The problem is that not all that many fossils have been found. That's because our distant ancestors lived in the jungle. Most of those ancestors were eaten up by predators. And if you get crushed in the jaws of a predator before ending up in their stomach and being pooped out in different places, there won't be any pretty fossils of you left behind. If, by some slim chance, you died in your sleep in one of those humid primeval forests, you'd instantly be gobbled up by all kinds of scavengers, big and small. There'd be nothing left. You'd only become a fossil if you somehow managed to die in a stagnant, muddy pond. Or if you were in a very dry desert and a thick layer of sand immediately covered you up. The chance of something like that happening is very small. But such fossils do exist.

ARE WE DESCENDED FROM LUCY?

Not many fossils of our ancestors have been found. Another problem is that there are too many different kinds of fossils. There's no nice, neat line from a mouse-like mammal via apes to humans. All kinds of different skulls and bones have been found of humanlike creatures that are quite different from us but aren't quite apes. Are they our ancestors? It's hard to say. In 1973, in Ethiopia, paleoanthropologist Donald Johanson and his assistant Tom Gray found a magnificent fossil of a 3.2-million-year-old woman. They called her Lucy because they liked listening to the Beatles song "Lucy in the Sky with Diamonds" in their camp. Lucy (and the other members of her species, who were found later) was about three feet, six inches tall.[3] She had the ribs of a chimpanzee and long arms and fingers, as all apes still do. She also had only a small brain. But . . . Lucy walked upright, just like a human.[4]

If you've been paying attention, you probably have two questions now. Number one: how can we tell from a few bones that Lucy once walked upright? And number two: why is walking upright so important?

LUCY'S MADE IT INTO THE NEXT ROUND OF 'SO YOU THINK YOU CAN WALK'!

How Can You Tell from a Skull That an Animal Once Walked Upright?

Paleontologists are used to finding small quantities of decayed remains. For that reason, they're delighted with even the tiniest little bone they find. Because even that can provide information. The length of the bone, the thickness, the layer of earth it was found in: these are all extra pieces of the puzzle of our past. Also, one bone can often count for two. If you find a bone from the left thumb, for instance, you automatically know what the right thumb looked like too: exactly the same but as a mirror image.

The same is true for every bone that we have twice. Even fragments of bones can give double the amount of information. If you find a piece of the left-hand side of the skull, you know what the right-hand side looked like. If you find just the left half of a skeleton, you know what the entire body would look like.

But a bone provides even more information than that. Something with long legs also has long leg bones. And an animal with lots of muscles needs thick bones. Imagine trying to lift a 200-pound weight with your massively strong muscles, while your arm bone's as thin a toothpick! The bone would snap in two. You can tell from the structure of a bone where the muscles were and how many there were. The shape of the bones indicates how an animal walked and what kind of posture it had. You can even work this out just from the skull alone. A skull has a hole in the bottom. It's where the backbone comes into your head. In people, that hole is nice and central. We walk upright and so have no need to use our head for balance. But our distant ancestors walked on four legs. For them it was more useful to have the hole closer to the back of the skull. That's better for crawling. But for Lucy there were other reasons to believe she walked upright. First of all, we know by 3.6-million-year-old footprints in volcanic ashes in Tanzania that there were already upright walking hominids in the same part of Africa. They had about the same feet as we do. But second and most important, the bones in her legs and knees have traits that belong to bipedality, or walking on two legs. Just as her pelvis and vertebrae do. So she probably walked upright.[5]

And Why Is Walking Upright So Important?

Walking upright is important in the evolution from ape to human. If we'd continued to walk on all fours, we wouldn't be as smart as we are now. Try to walk on all fours, like an ape does, for a mile. What an awful thought! But walking on your two feet for a mile is no problem at all. So just simply walking like a chimp takes a lot more effort and energy.

Large brains also use a lot of energy. Lucy's brain was just a quarter the size of ours. But 10 percent of her energy went straight to her brain. Human brains use twice as much energy as Lucy's, but animal brains use far less.[6] Walking on all fours *and* having a large brain isn't a good combination. It means you have to find a huge amount of food, and that's not easy. If you can run, it's a lot easier to hunt for animals. Apes can run, and they're quick too, but they can't do it for long. After a short sprint, they're exhausted. Some humans can run for hours at a time. For hunting, you really need stamina. You have to cover miles, searching for traces of animals. And when you find them, you have to chase them.

How Did We Get Smart by Getting Smarter?

By walking upright, our ancestors used less energy. That way, they could afford to have an energy-guzzling brain without suddenly needing to find lots of extra food. The larger brain also made them smarter and smarter. They started to make weapons and tools, like spears and knives. That made them better at hunting and meant they could get more meat from an animal's bones. So they could also consume more food, which in turn made it possible for them to have even larger brains. One thing led to another. Our ancestors really needed those big brains, because it was a difficult time to survive. Those who were smarter had a much greater chance of finding enough to eat and of leaving descendants. And that's how our ancestors were able to become such clever creatures in a relatively short time.[7]

WILL APES EVER BECOME AS SMART AS US?

Apes can use tools such as stones and twigs. But those stones and twigs are ready-made tools. They can't make an ax from the things around them, as early humans were able to do. The cleverest ape on Earth is the bonobo Kanzi.[8] Kanzi can use a special symbolic language to talk to humans. He points at pictures that have their own meaning. If he presses the buttons that mean *ball*, *play*, and *Kanzi*, you know he wants to play with the ball. You can also ask him questions, and he answers. Kanzi knows hundreds of words, and he understands a huge amount. He can solve puzzles and even play computer games. He's better at Pac-Man than I am.[9]

But can he make his own tools? No, that's something Kanzi will never learn. Not even if a person first demonstrates how to turn a stone into an ax. Bonobos are lacking that part of the brain that allows them to think about

DRYOPITHECUS • AUSTRALOPITHECUS • HOMO ERECTUS • HOMO NEANDERTHALENSIS • HOMO SAPIENS

how to bang one stone against another to make a sharp edge.[10] Lucy would probably not quite have been able to do it either. And yet stone tools have been found that are around 2.9 million years old. So she wasn't far off.[11]

What Fossils Have Been Found?

Lucy isn't the only fossil, of course. The oldest fossil with human characteristics was found in the desert in Chad: *Sahelanthropus tchadensis*. It is far older than Lucy but already had a combination of apelike and humanlike features. The small brain, sloping face, and prominent brow ridges make it look like an ape. The teeth and spinal cord opening underneath the skull resemble a human's. Scientists believe *Sahelanthropus tchadensis* to be between 6 million and 7 million years old. But is it one of our ancestors?[12]

In Africa, fossils from 1.5 million years ago have been found, of *Homo ergaster*, the "working man." These were humanlike creatures around six feet tall. They had long legs and short arms, toes, and fingers. Just like a human. Their brains were about two-thirds the size of ours. And they made their own tools. But were they our ancestors?[13]

Lots of fossils of *Homo erectus*, the "upright man," have also been found. The oldest examples had brains the size of *Homo ergaster*'s brain, and over the course of time their brains became larger and larger, but they still weren't as big as modern humans' brains. They were also around six feet tall and were excellent at running. And of course they could make their own tools. But were they our ancestors?[14]

Finally, fossils have been found of a humanlike species that was very similar to us: *Homo neanderthalensis*. These "Neanderthals" were a little smaller, hugely muscular (they'd win almost every gold medal in the Olympic Games), and intelligent. Their brains were just as big as ours, or even bigger. Could they have been our ancestors?[15]

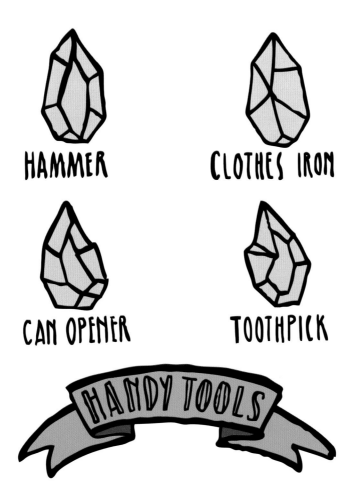

HAMMER

CLOTHES IRON

CAN OPENER

TOOTHPICK

HANDY TOOLS

Why Do We Still Know So Little, in Spite of All Those Fossils?

Back to the Schmo family and their rockets. It's very easy to draw a family tree for them. The trunk starts with Joe Schmo and moves on to Joe Schmo Jr. And there are side branches for Mo and Tony Schmo. They split again until finally there's a whole tree. Every branch comes from the first Joe Schmo. But not every branch comes from Mo Schmo. If you see a To-schmo rocket, you know it's one of Tony's, not Mo's.

With the human family tree, it's a lot more difficult. Fossils don't have signs on them saying *To-schmo* or *Jo-schmo*. We know that somewhere along the line we're distant relatives of all those humanlike fossils. But are they in the line that leads directly to us? We don't know. Also, you can't draw any definite conclusions from a single fossil. Imagine if creatures in the future found a fossil of a two-toed person from the Vadoma tribe or one of those little people from Ecuador. Maybe they'd see it as a completely different species from the humans, even though they're just normal people. Or they could think that they were the only kind of people on Earth. Very little about our past is certain.

HAVE SCIENTISTS DISCOVERED EVE?

There are plenty of questions about our past. But there are also lots of interesting things to say about what we do know. For example, the oldest fossils of modern humans, *Homo sapiens*, are about 195,000 years old.[16] *Homo erectus* fossils are between 1.89 million and 143,000 years old, and the Neanderthal ones are between 180,000 and 30,000 years old.[17] For centuries, all these humanlike species lived on Earth at the same time! Are we descended from

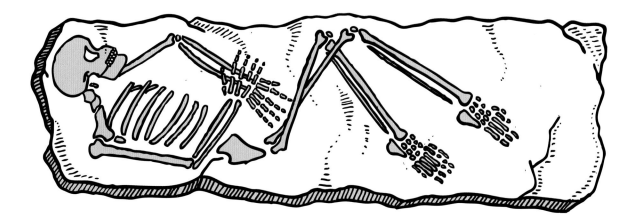

them? That's quite possible. After all, humans are descended from slime eels, and slime eels are still around. Not all of the species that were among our ancestors have become extinct.

Do You Have Neanderthal Blood?

We also know that fossils from around a million years ago to half a million years ago are all from *Homo erectus* or *Homo heidelbergensis*. *Homo heidelbergensis* was the first human-like species to live in a colder climate. It had a short and muscular body that was well capable of conserving heat. A bit like that of a Neanderthal, so that's why scientists think it might be Neanderthal's ancestor. Perhaps *erectus* and *heidelbergensis* were the only humanlike species at that time.[18] It was a difficult period with lots of climate changes. There were so few ancient peoples back then that they came very close to extinction. We very nearly might not have existed at all. As most fossils from that period are from *Homo erectus*, there's a good chance we're descended from them. We also know that modern humans and Neanderthals lived in the same region. They lived so closely in Europe and Asia that they probably had children together. Some of us may have some Neanderthal in us. Except if your ancestors are from Africa. Neanderthals didn't live there.[19]

The paleontologists' work is nowhere near done. Every year there are new pieces in the puzzle, giving us more information about our past. A few years ago, for instance, on the Indonesian island of Flores, researchers found yet another species of human, *Homo floresiensis*. And it was a species that lived until fairly recently. These creatures became extinct only about 12,000 years ago, but they were less like us than the Neanderthals were.[20] They were far smaller than us, and they had small brains, even though they would have been far more intelligent than apes. While their brains may have been small, they looked exactly like ours in every other respect. And who knows what discoveries will be made in the coming years? But no matter what kind of bones scientists find, they still won't be able to provide definitive proof of our origins. Unless a complete fossilized skeleton from each ancestor is found with an arrow pointing to the next one . . . we will likely never know.

Did Eve Exist?

Luckily, there's also DNA, which still has plenty of secrets to reveal. For example, in recent years, scientists from the University of California, Berkeley, carried out a major new study. They compared the DNA of hundreds of people on Earth. What kinds of differences were there? And what could those differences tell us? Their conclusion was remarkable. The DNA of all the people on Earth shows huge similarities. From the Aboriginal people of Australia to the Inuit of the Canadian Arctic and everyone in between—we're all distant cousins.

And the scientists made another discovery. The DNA was so similar that they were able to work out that everyone on Earth must be descended from just one woman. A woman who lived in Africa around 200,000 years ago.[21] So did Eve actually exist? Well, yes and no, because the scientists immediately named her Eve, even though there's a very slim chance that was actually her name. Unlike the Bible story, this woman was certainly not the only woman on Earth at the time, and she had a mother and father, just the same as everyone else. Of course, we also descend from the mother, father, and grandparents of Eve, but she is the youngest ancestor whose DNA can be found in all humans today.

What Will Our Distant Grandchildren Look Like?

We know a bit about the past. But what about the future? Can we predict what human beings will look like in thousands of years' time? Up until now, our brain has just gotten bigger and better. Will our great-grandchildren be smarter than us? There's no guarantee. In the time when Eve lived, it was a big advantage to be smarter than other people. The weakest didn't survive. Now we live in an age where less intelligent people can also survive. They may not become a professor or a bank manager, but they're not going to die of starvation before passing on their genes either.

In some ways, we actually make less use of our brains these days. We leave math to our calculators. We use GPS devices to find our way. We don't even have to remember telephone numbers anymore. Perhaps our distant descendants will actually turn out to be dumber than us . . .

IS THERE LIFE ON OTHER PLANETS? AND WHAT DOES IT LOOK LIKE?

This book has been almost entirely about life on Earth. It might be fun to take a quick look farther afield. What about life on other planets? Does it exist? And, if so, what does it look like? With hundreds of billions of galaxies, many with hundreds of billions of stars, some of which have a handful of planets scattered around them, there's hardly any question about whether extraterrestrial life exists. What's more interesting is the question of what

our distant "neighbors" might look like. And according to biologists, there are a few conclusions we can draw.

If these neighbors are in our own galaxy, then we actually know a considerable amount. Mars could only ever have been inhabited by bacteria-like creatures. One, because Mars does not have a protective atmosphere like Earth's. And two, because Martian soil contains much less organic matter than Earth soil. There's simply not enough food for larger life-forms.[22] But there is potential for life on the moon Europa, which orbits Jupiter. That moon is covered with a thick layer of ice. There could be an ocean beneath

the ice, heated by a volcanic core. That would allow a real food chain to exist, with predators, prey, bacteria, and plants. And there would have to be a top predator—the equivalent of the Earth's great white shark. It would have to be a very small great white shark, though. Europa's not very big, so the shark could only be the size of a bay shrimp at most.[23]

Why Are Space Aliens Probably Carnivores?

There's a good chance that alien life-forms are a lot like worms. A wormlike form has proven successful on Earth for hundreds of millions of years. It could very well also occur on unknown planets like Gnork III, Zruuut, or Rksjpgpwt too. And if there's light on these planets, there's a fair chance that the inhabitants have eyes. A minimum of two eyes is useful for perceiving depth and judging distances. Creatures that work together in swarms or colonies, like our ants and bees, are also a possibility.

It's likely that the space aliens will be predators. Generally, predators are a little smarter than herbivores. Predators have to rely on their intelligence to survive. A deer or a gazelle has more escape strategies than a cauliflower. We'll have to make sure the space aliens don't eat us up if we ever meet.

Could Space Aliens Live to the Age of 10,000?

Strange creatures with glass-like veins full of sulfuric acid or boiling cyanide are also a possibility. What's toxic on our planet could turn out to be the most essential component for life elsewhere. You could even encounter single-celled creatures that are the size of blue whales. On extremely cold planets, chemical reactions occur more slowly. Creatures that live there grow a lot older than we do. An elderly inhabitant of an ice planet could very well have to blow out 10,000 candles on his birthday cake.

And yet it's most likely that they'll be creatures like the ones on Earth, with eyes, organs, limbs, and skin or fur. If a new planet like Earth were to start forming, it would probably end up with inhabitants similar to the ones on our own planet. Maybe somewhere far, far away there's someone living who looks like Joe Schmo from Buffalo. There could even be someone who looks like you . . .

AND ONE LAST THING . . .

Evolution is a sensitive subject. When strict believers and scientists discuss who's right, the debate often becomes very heated. You might think I'd side with the scientists who don't believe in God, but that's not entirely the case.

It's true that I don't believe the Earth was created in six days or that the universe is just a few thousand years old. But still I think it's a strange idea that everything around us could have just appeared from nowhere. So is there a god? I don't know. There are scientists who are far more intelligent than me who believe in God. It's perfectly possible to believe in both evolution and God at the same time. There are also scientists who are far more intelligent than me who don't believe in God. One thing is certain: I'm too dumb to answer the question about whether there's a god or not. And I actually think that goes for all of us.

Just think about it. If there's no god, where does everything around us come from? How did it all get there? And if there is a god, where did that god come from?

Can You Tell from a Person's Brain If He's Religious?

I grew up in a religious family and a remnant of that belief has stayed with me. You could say I still believe with my heart but not with my head. But a professor told me that belief is actually situated in our brains. He can see from someone's brain if that person is religious or not! Brain scientists made scans of brains of religious people while they were thinking about God. The scientists could see there was a lot happening in the brain that wouldn't happen with nonreligious people. The temporal lobe is one part of the brain that was particularly active during those scans of religious people. If you stimulate a specific part of the temporal lobe with electric currents, then people who stopped believing in God long ago become believers again. Ex-Christians see Jesus or God. Former Muslims see Mohammed or Allah. And people who were brought up as Buddhists see Buddha. The geneticist Dean Hamer discovered a gene that determines the level of our "talent" for

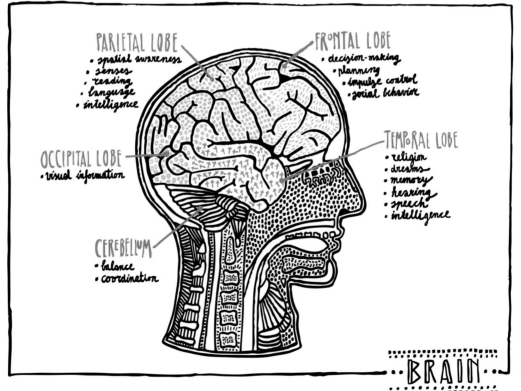

PARIETAL LOBE
• spatial awareness
• senses
• reading
• language
• intelligence

FRONTAL LOBE
• decision-making
• planning
• impulse control
• social behavior

OCCIPITAL LOBE
• visual information

TEMPORAL LOBE
• religion
• dreams
• memory
• hearing
• speech
• intelligence

CEREBELLUM
• balance
• coordination

BRAIN

24

believing. This gene controls a protein that is crucial for several important functions of the brain. There are probably more genes like this one. I guess some of them in my DNA are switched to "religion on," since there's still a bit of religiousness in me while science gives me no reason to believe.[25]

There's not an inch of me that doubts evolution, but as I was doing my research for this book, I often wondered if absolutely everything the scientists claim is really true. Sometimes I read articles that sparked doubts about the scientific theories. I also kept coming across articles written by the creationists, the people who believe that God made the Earth. What was interesting was that they didn't really lie in their articles. Almost everything in them was true. The only problem was that the writers didn't provide all of the information. Like in the chapter about the bombardier beetle. Not one of the articles I read by creationists stated that there are hundreds of kinds of beetles with the same "explosive" substances in their back. A few half-truths quickly add up to a whole lie.

Do Scientists Conceal the Facts?

Strangely enough, some creationists accuse scientists of concealing and distorting information. But that's something I didn't come across in any of my investigations. In fact, I think that many atheist scientists would prefer to believe in God. Imagine being able to live forever in heaven after you die. Wouldn't that be great? And imagine, as a scientist, being able to prove that God exists, in the same way you can prove that the Earth orbits the sun. You'd win the Nobel Prize and eternal fame. But that proof has never been found, and it's probably impossible to find.

What should you do with this information? That's entirely up to you. If you're struggling with the question of whether God exists, you can go looking for more information, from the religious people and the scientists. Then you can decide for yourself what you believe. Even if it's just that you simply don't know. If you're excited by what you read, read more. Learn as much as you can about life on Earth, and who our neighbors might be in the rest of the galaxy and beyond. Perhaps evolution will end up making people smarter and smarter. There will always be more mysteries to solve. It will take a lot of big brains, the brains that took millions of years to evolve and that are still evolving, to solve them.

NOTES

JUST A QUICK WORD BEFORE WE REALLY GET STARTED

1. Bradley Voytek, "Are There Really as Many Neurons in the Human Brain as Stars in the Milky Way?", May 20, 2013, http://www.nature.com/scitable/blog/brain-metrics /are_there_really_as_many

1. MARVELS, MYSTERIES, AND YOU

1. David Ferucci, "Henrik Schärfe: Inventor," *Time*, April 18, 2012, http://content.time .com/time/specials/packages/article/0,28804,2111975_2111976 _2111965,00.html.

2. Bianconi et al, "An Estimation of the Number of Cells in the Human Body," 471.

3. "How Stem Cells Turn into Skin Cells: A Small RNA, miR-203, Is Critical for Skin Creation," Tech Museum of Innovation, March 7, 2008, http://genetics.thetech.org /original_news/news79.

4. James Randerson, "How Many Neurons Make a Human Brain? Billions Fewer than We Thought," *Guardian*, February 28, 2012, http://www.theguardian.com/science /blog/2012/feb/28/how-many-neurons-human-brain.

5. Associated Press, "Study: Even Healthy Humans Can Host 10,000 Microbe Species," CBSNews.com, June 13, 2012, http://www.cbsnews.com/news/study-even -healthy-humans-can-host-10000-microbe-species.

6. Jessica Hamzelou, "Babies Are Born Dirty, with a Gutful of Bacteria," *New Scientist*, April 12, 2012, http://www.newscientist.com/article/mg21428603.800-babies-are-born -dirty-with-a-gutful-of-bacteria.html.

7. "Microbial Star Trekkers Survive 553 Days in Space," *Discovery News*, February 11, 2013, http://news.discovery.com/space/record-breaking-microbial-star-trekkers.htm.

8. *Ecomare*, s.v. "Reproduction of Fish," accessed July 7, 2014, http://www.ecomare.nl /en/encyclopedia/organisms/animals/fish/fish-biology/reproduction-of-fish.

9. *MedlinePlus*, s.v. "Cell Division," last modified November 20, 2012, http://www.nlm .nih.gov/medlineplus/ency/anatomyvideos/000025.htm.

10. Sally Pobojewski, "The First 21 Days: Risk and Mystery Surround the Embryo's Earliest Development," *Medicine at Michigan* 10, no. 1 (Spring 2008), http://www .medicineatmichigan.org/magazine/2008/spring/21days.

11. *Lifebeat*, s.v. "How Your Heart Works," April 2012, http://www .bostonscientific.com/lifebeat-online/heart-smart/how-your-heart-works.html.

12. *MedlinePlus*, s.v. "Fetal Development, Week by Week Changes," last modified May 16, 2014, http://www.nlm.nih.gov/medlineplus/ency/article/002398.htm.

13. Sandra Ackerman, *Discovering the Brain* (Washington, DC: The National Academies Press, 1992), 86, http://www.nap.edu/openbook.php?record_id =1785&page=86.

14. *Egypt Art Site*, s.v. "Ptah, the Opener," accessed July 7, 2014, http://www .egyptartsite.com/ptah.html.

15. *Myths Encyclopedia*, s.v. "Popol Vuh," accessed July 8, 2014, http://www .mythencyclopedia.com/Pa-Pr/Popol-Vuh.html.

2. HOW OLD IS THE EARTH?

1. Donald Simanek, "Bishop Ussher Dates the World: 4004 BC," accessed July 10, 2014, http://www.lhup.edu/~dsimanek/ussher.htm.

2. Arthur Stinner, "Calculating the Age of the Earth and the Sun," *Physics Education* 37, July 2002, 296, http://www.phy.duke.edu/~hsg/134/lectures/ages-of-earth-sun.pdf.

3. Simanek, "Bishop Ussher Dates the World: 4004 BC."

4. "Creation of Heaven and Earth by Pangu," Cultural China, accessed July 10, 2014, http://www.cultural-china.com/chinaWH/html/en/13Traditions268.html.

5. "Hindu Cosmology," Hindu Wisdom, accessed July 10, 2014, http://www .hinduwisdom.info/Hindu_Cosmology.htm.

6. Gary Dean Johnson, "James Hutton's Recognition of the Geologic Cycle," in *Encyclopædia Britannica Online*, last modified February 2, 2014, http://www.britannica .com/EBchecked/topic/229486/geochronology/70044/The-emergence-of-modern -geologic-thought.

7. "Mountain Ranges," *Plate Tectonics*, accessed July 11, 2014, http://www.platetectonics
.com/book/page_11.asp.

8. "James Hutton: The Founder of Modern Geology," American Museum of Natural
History, accessed July 11, 2014, http://www.amnh.org/education/resources/rfl/web
/essaybooks/earth/p_hutton.html.

9. *Foundational Concepts*, s.v. "Extinction," Smithsonian National Museum of Natural
History, accessed July 9, 2014, http://paleobiology.si.edu/geotime/main/foundation
_life4.html.

10. James Tobin, "Alamo Breccia 2011," *Meteorite Times Magazine*, December 1, 2011,
http://www.meteorite-times.com/jims-fragments/alamo-breccia-2011.

11. *Geologic Time*, art, from *Encyclopædia Britannica Online*, accessed July 4, 2014,
http://www.britannica.com/media/full/66800.

12. "Half Lives," Integrated Environmental Management, Inc., accessed July 11, 2014,
http://www.iem-inc.com/information/tools/half-lives.

13. Robert Roy Britt, "Crusty Old Discovery Reveals Early Earth's History,"
LiveScience, March 23, 2007, http://www.livescience.com/7207-crusty-discovery
-reveals-early-earth-history.html.

14. Fraser Cain, "What Is the Evidence for the Big Bang?," Universe Today, November
18, 2013, http://www.universetoday.com/106498/what-is-the-evidence-for-the-big-bang.

15. Ibid.

16. "Speed of Light vs Speed of Sound," Cosmicopia, accessed July 10, 2014, http://
helios.gsfc.nasa.gov/qa_gp_ls.html#lightsound.

17. "The Nearest Star," NASA's HEASARC, accessed July 11, 2014, http://heasarc.gsfc
.nasa.gov/docs/cosmic/nearest_star_info.html.

18. Rebecca Morelle, "New Galaxy 'Most Distant' Yet Discovered," BBC News,
October 23, 2013, http://www.bbc.com/news/science-environment-24637890.

3. THE HISTORY OF EVERYTHING IN 1,620 WORDS

1. Dan Vergano, "Big Bang's 'Smoking Gun' Confirms Early Universe's Exponential
Growth," *National Geographic*, March 17, 2014, http://news.nationalgeographic.com
/news/2014/14/140317-big-bang-gravitational-waves-inflation-science-space.

2. Ibid.

3. "How Are Stars Formed, and How Do They End Up?," NASA's Imagine the Universe, accessed July 12, 2014, http://imagine.gsfc.nasa.gov/docs/ask_astro/answers/970422f.html.

4. "New Study Proves Moon Was Created in Massive Planetary Collision," Phys.org, October 17, 2012, http://phys.org/news/2012-10-massive-planetary-collision-zapped-key.html.

5. Tobias Chant Owen, *Encyclopædia Britannica Online*, s.v. "Solar System," last modified August 12, 2014, http://www.britannica.com/EBchecked/topic/553008/solar-system.

6. Lisa Grossman, "Fast-Spinning Earth Settles Mystery of Moon's Make-Up," *New Scientist*, October 17, 2012, http://www.newscientist.com/article/dn22393-fastspinning-earth-settles-mystery-of-moons-makeup.html#.U8UOA1YmXUY.

7. Brian Greene, "How Did Water Come to Earth?," *Smithsonian Magazine*, May 2013, http://www.smithsonianmag.com/science-nature/how-did-water-come-to-earth-72037248/?no-ist.

8. "Evolutionary Developmental Biology Lecture 7," Faculty of Biological Sciences, University of Leeds, accessed July 12, 2014, http://www.leeds.ac.uk/chb/lectures/edb07.html.

9. "Timeline of Evolution," CK-12, accessed July 13, 2014, http://www.ck12.org/book/CK-12-Life-Science-Concepts-For-Middle-School/section/4.13.

4. THE GREATEST SCIENTIFIC IDEA OF ALL TIME

1. F. J. Sulloway, "Darwin and His Finches: The Evolution of a Legend," *Journal of the History of Biology* 15, no. 1 (1982): 1–53, www.sulloway.org/Finches.pdf.

2. "Darwin's Timeline," AboutDarwin.com, accessed July 13, 2014, http://www.aboutdarwin.com/timeline/time_01.html.

3. Richard Dawkins, *The Greatest Show on Earth: The Evidence for Evolution* (New York, Free Press, 2009), 399.

4. "All Species Share a Common Descent," DarwinWasRight.org, accessed July 13, 2014, http://www.darwinwasright.org/common_descent.html.

5. Wesley R. Elsberry, "A Sesquicentennial: Wallace and Darwin at the Linnean Society," *The Austringer* (blog), June 30, 2008, http://austringer.net/wp/index.php/2008/06/30/a-sesquicentennial-wallace-and-darwin-at-the-linnean-society.

6. Jane R. Camerini, "Alfred Russel Wallace," in *Encyclopædia Brittannica Online*, last modified July 21, 2014, http://www.britannica.com/EBchecked/topic/634738/Alfred-Russel-Wallace.

5. EVOLUTION IN BRIEF

1. "Evolution," History World, accessed July 15, 2014, http://www.historyworld.net/wrldhis/PlainTextHistories.asp?historyid=aa34.

2. Richard Turner, "Darwin's Moth: 'Proof of Evolution,'" BBC, April 6, 2008, last modified January 26, 2009, http://www.bbc.co.uk/manchester/content/articles/2008/06/04/040608_peppered_moth_feature.shtml.

3. Don Thompson, "Redwoods Siphon Water from the Top and Bottom," *Los Angeles Times*, September 1, 2002, http://articles.latimes.com/2002/sep/01/news/adme-redwoods1.

4. Mike Hansell, *Built by Animals: The National History of Animal Architecture* (Oxford: Oxford University Press, 2007), 218.

5. Dawkins, *The Greatest Show on Earth*, 60–62, 64.

6. Francisco Jose Ayala, "Sexual Selection," in *Encyclopædia Brittannica Online*, last modified September 13, 2012, http://www.britannica.com/EBchecked/topic/537205/sexual-selection.

7. Jared Diamond, "Animal Art: Variation in Bower Decorating Style among Male Bowerbirds *Amblyornis inornatus*," *Proceedings of the National Academy of Sciences of the United States of America* 83 (December 30, 1985): 3042–6, http://www.pnas.org/content/83/9/3042.full.pdf.

8. Rosie Mestel, "Animal Attraction's Practical Purpose," *Los Angeles Times*, July 9, 2001, http://articles.latimes.com/2001/jul/09/news/mn-20315.

9. Stephen Jay Gould, *Ever Since Darwin: Reflections in Natural History* (New York: W. W. Norton and Company, 1992), 84–85.

10. Desmond Morris, *The Naked Ape: A Zoologist's Study of the Human Animal* (New York: Random House, 1967), 50–103.

11. Markus Jokela, "Physical Attractiveness and Reproductive Success in Humans: Evidence from the Late 20th Century United States," *Evolution and Human Behavior*, last modified March 23, 2009, http://blogs.helsinki.fi/mmjokela/files/2009/07/jokela_attractiveness_fertility_ehb.pdf.

12. Bjorn Carey, "The Rules of Attraction in the Game of Love," LiveScience, February 13, 2006, http://www.livescience.com/7023-rules-attraction-game-love.html.

6. ALL ABOUT THE FAMILY

1. Tanya Lewis, "How Queen Bees Reign over Reproduction," LiveScience, January 16, 2014, http://www.livescience.com/42629-queen-insects-signal-worker-infertility.html.

2. "Born to Run, How Our Genes Affect Our Sporting Talent," July 31, 2012, http://www.euronews.com/2012/07/31/born-to-run-how-our-genes-affect-our-sporting-talent.

3. Richard Dawkins, *The Selfish Gene: 30th Anniversary Edition* (Oxford: Oxford University Press, 2006).

7. HOW LIFE ON EARTH BEGAN

1. Sid Perkins, "Long-Neglected Experiment Gives New Clues to Origin of Life," *Science*, March 21, 2011, http://news.sciencemag.org/2011/03/long-neglected -experiment-gives-new-clues-origin-life?ref=hp.

2. "What Are Proteins and What Do They Do?," Genetics Home Reference, last modified August 25, 2014, http://ghr.nlm.nih.gov/handbook/howgeneswork/protein.

3. Perkins, "Long-Neglected Experiment Gives New Clues to Origin of Life."

4. "Miller/Urey Experiment," Cruising Chemestry, accessed September 10, 2014, http://people.chem.duke.edu/~jds/cruise_chem/Exobiology/miller.html.

5. "DNA," Home Science Tools newsletter, accessed July 14, 2014, http://www .hometrainingtools.com/a/dna.

6. Kara Rogers, "The Origin of Life in an RNA World," *Encyclopædia Britannica Blog*, May 15, 2009, http://www.britannica.com/blogs/2009/05/the-origin-of-life-in-an-rna -world.

7. Videojug, "How to Make Your Own Salt Crystals," YouTube video, 3:09, posted by "Two-Point-Four," March, 9 2012, http://www.youtube.com/watch?v=9zoh-COQAQM.

8. Michael Marshall, "Biologists Create Self-Replicating RNA Molecule," *New Scientist*, April, 7 2011, http://www.newscientist.com/blogs/shortsharpscience/2011/04 /rna-enzyme-makes-another-rna-e.html.

9. "Fatty Acids," Exploring Life's Origins, accessed July 16, 2014, http:// exploringorigins.org/fattyacids.html.

10. Dana Coulter, "What's Hitting Earth?" Science@NASA, March 1, 2011, http://science.nasa.gov/science-news/science-at-nasa/2011/01mar_meteornetwork.

11. "How Much Does Earth Weigh and How Is This Measured?" Cool Cosmos, accessed July 15, 2014, http://coolcosmos.ipac.caltech.edu/ask/61-How-much-does-Earth-weigh-and-how-is-this-measured-.

12. Anne M. Stark, "It's a Shock: Life on Earth May Have Come from out of This World," Lawrence Livermore National Laboratory, accessed July 30, 2014, https://www.llnl.gov/news/newsreleases/2013/Sep/NR-13-09-04.html#.U9jQPFYmXUZ.

8. SURVIVING IN THE PRIMEVAL OCEANS

1. "The First Life on Earth," Smithsonian National Museum of Natural History, accessed July 16, 2014, http://paleobiology.si.edu/geotime/main/htmlversion/archean3.html.

2. Colin Schultz, "The Center of the Earth Is as Hot as the Sun," Smithsonian.com, April 26, 2013, http://www.smithsonianmag.com/smart-news/the-center-of-the-earth-is-as-hot-as-the-sun-43631207/?no-ist.

3. "Geothermal Areas Around the World," accessed July 16, 2014, http://www.greenibis.com/edu/geo/frames/where.html.

4. Gemma Elwin Harris, ed., *Big Questions from Little People Answered by Some Very Big People* (London: Faber and Faber, 2012), 195–196.

5. Yellowstone National Park staff, "Life in Extreme Heat," Yellowstone Resources and Issues Handbook 2014, 119–120, accessed September 10, 2014, http://www.nps.gov/yell/planyourvisit/upload/RI_2014_07_Thermophiles.pdf; "Digestive System," accessed July 30, 2014, http://biology.clc.uc.edu/courses/bio105/digestiv.htm.

6. Ben Waggoner and Brian Speer, "Introduction to the Archaea: Life's Extremists . . . ," University of California Museum of Paleontology, accessed July 17, 2014, http://www.ucmp.berkeley.edu/archaea/archaea.html.

7. Stephen Hart, "Cave Slime," *Astrobiology Magazine*, June 30, 2003, http://www.nasa.gov/vision/universe/solarsystem/cave_slime.html.

8. DOE/Lawrence Berkeley National Laboratory, "Chemical Changes in Cells Tracked as They Endure Extreme Conditions," ScienceDaily, July 16 2009, http://www.sciencedaily.com/releases/2009/07/090707142140.htm.

9. Brandon Keim, "Life Thrives in Earth's Most Mars-Like Environment," *Wired*, March 3, 2009, http://www.wired.com/2009/03/nearmarslife.

10. "History of Life on Earth," BBC, accessed July 18, 2014, http://www.bbc.co.uk /nature/history_of_the_earth.

11. The Open University, s.v. "Stromatolites," accessed July 16, 2014, http://www.open .ac.uk/earth-research/tindle/AGT/AGT_Home_2010/RMS-Info-Stromatolite.html.

12. University of Zurich, "Great Oxidation Event: More Oxygen through Multicellularity," ScienceDaily, January 17, 2013, http://www.sciencedaily.com /releases/2013/01/130117084856.htm.

13. Ker Than, "All Species Evolved from Single Cell, Study Finds," *National Geographic News*, May 13, 2010, last modified May 14, 2010, http://news.nationalgeographic.com /news/2010/05/100513-science-evolution-darwin-single-ancestor.

14. Harvey Lodish, Arnold Berk, S. Lawrence Zipursky, Paul Matsudaira, David Baltimore, and James Darnell, *Molecular Cell Biology* (New York, W. H. Freeman, 2000), section 22.3.

15. Australian National University, "Six Easy Lessons in Sea Sponges," ScienceAlert, June 8, 2008, http://www.sciencealert.com.au/features/20080906-17456.html.

16. Michael Gunton et al., *Journey of Life* (BBC/Discovery Channel coproduction, 2005).

17. "Twenty-Four Eyes but No Brain," Earth History, accessed July 16, 2014, http:// www.earthhistory.org.uk/corals-and-jellies/box-jellyfish.

18. Wolfgang Sefarth, "Regeneration," Marine Flatworms of the World, accessed July 17, 2014, http://www.rzuser.uni-heidelberg.de/~bu6/Introduction03.html.

19. "Calories in Peanut Butter and Jelly Sandwich," Calorie Count, accessed July 15, 2014, http://caloriecount.about.com/calories-yours-truly-peanut-butter-jelly-i68200.

20. Jenifer Nadeau, "Pasture: Evaluation and Management of Existing Pasture," University of Connecticut, accessed July 15, 2014, http://animalscience.uconn.edu /extension/publications/pastureexist.htm; *Africa Guide*, s.v. "African Lion," accessed July 15, 2014, http://www.africaguide.com/wildlife/lion.htm.

21. "Strange Creatures—A Burgess Shale Fossil Sampler," Smithsonian National Museum of Natural History, accessed July 16, 2014, http://paleobiology.si.edu/burgess.

22. Ibid.

23. "Vendian Animals: *Kimberella*," University of California Museum of Paleontology, accessed July 16, 2014, http://www.ucmp.berkeley.edu/vendian/kimberella.html.

24. Alexander M. Kerr, "Holothuroidea, Sea Cucumbers," Tree of Life Web Project, accessed July 16, 2014, http://tolweb.org/Holothuroidea.

25. "Strange Creatures—A Burgess Shale Fossil Sampler."

26. "Evolution: First Life," *BBC Wildlife Magazine*, December 10, 2010, http://www.discoverwildlife.com/animals/evolution-first-life.

27. "Strange Creatures—A Burgess Shale Fossil Sampler."

28. Anthony J King, "Evolution and Directions to Killarney," *Cosmos*, April 30, 2012, http://ska.cosmosmagazine.com/blog/evolution-and-directions-killarney.

29. University of Arkansas, Fayetteville, "Shell-Shock: Three University of Arkansas Students Find World's Longest Nautiloid Fossil," ScienceDaily, January 27, 2003, http://www.sciencedaily.com/releases/2003/01/030127075642.htm.

30. Benjamin Cummings, art, from "Morphologies, Life History, and Taxonomy of Tunicates," Clark University, 2006, http://www.clarku.edu/departments/biology/biol201/2006/mtrivette/morphologies.htm.

31. Patrick Lemaire, "Evolutionary Crossroads in Developmental Biology: The Tunicates," *Development*, accessed July 16, 2014, http://dev.biologists.org/content/138/11/2143.full; "Vase Tunicate, *Ciona intestinalis*," redOrbit, accessed July 16, 2014, http://www.redorbit.com/education/reference_library/animal_kingdom/miscellaneuos/1112520747/vase-tunicate-ciona-intestinalis.

32. Taihung Duong, "Embryology," Indiana University School of Medicine, accessed July 16, 2014, http://web.indstate.edu/thcme/duong/EMBRYOL.html.

33. David Denning and Bruce J. Russell, "Branches on the Tree of Life: Chordates," BioMedia Assocaites, accessed July 16, 2014, https://www.ebiomedia.com/branches-on-the-tree-of-life-chordates.html.

34. Tia Ghose, "Megalodon Mystery: What Killed Earth's Largest Shark?," LiveScience, November 4, 2013, http://www.livescience.com/40920-megalodon-got-too-big-extinction.html.

9. HALF HUMAN, HALF FISH

1. "First Land Plants and Fungi Changed Earth's Climate, Paving the Way for Explosive Evolution of Land Animals, New Gene Study Suggests," Penn State Eberly College of Science, accessed July 17, 2014, http://science.psu.edu/news-and-events/2001-news/Hedges8-2001.htm.

2. Norman Green, "Crustacean Profile Common Woodlouse," Sciences 360, June 7, 2011, http://www.sciences360.com/index.php/crustacean-profile-common-woodlouse-5483.

3. Neil Shubin, *Your Inner Fish: A Journey into the 3.5-Billion-Year History of the Human Body* (New York: Random House, 2008), 33.

4. Dawkins, *The Greatest Show on Earth*, 366.

5. James Owen, "Walking Began Underwater, Strolling-Fish Discovery Suggests," *National Geographic News*, December 13, 2011, http://news.nationalgeographic.com /news/2011/12/111213-walking-fish-walk-lungfish-science-lungfish.

6. Shubin, *Your Inner Fish*, 3–27.

7. *Fossil Record: Geologic Time Scale with Major Evolutionary Events*, art, from *Encyclopædia Britannica Online*, last modified August 8, 2014, http://www.britannica .com/EBchecked/topic/229694/geologic-time.

8. USGS, "Plate Tectonics—Pangaea Continent Maps," art, from Geology.com, accessed July 18, 2014, http://geology.com/pangea.htm.

9. J. Floor Anthoni, *Continental Drift*, art, from "Oceanography: Oceans, Continental Drift and the Origins of the Oceans," Seafriends, 2000, http://www.seafriends.org.nz /oceano/oceans.htm.

10. Jessica Vrazilek, "Study: North Pole Once Was Tropical," CBS News, May 31, 2006, http://www.cbsnews.com/news/study-north-pole-once-was-tropical.

11. Lawrence Osborne, "The Fossil Frenzy," *New York Times Magazine*, October 29, 2000, http://partners.nytimes.com/library/magazine/home/20001029mag-fossil.html.

12. "Why the Cliffs Exist," Joggins Fossil, accessed July 16, 2014, http:// jogginsfossilcliffs.net/cliffs/why.

13. "Mountain Ranges."

14. Shubin, *Your Inner Fish*.

15. Dawkins, *The Greatest Show on Earth*, 167–8.

16. "Ancient Amphibians," Zoological Society of London, accessed July 16, 2014, http://www.edgeofexistence.org/amphibian_conservation/ancient_amphibians.php.

17. "*Tiktaalik roseae*—Missing Link Fossil: When Fins Became Limbs," age-of-the-sage .org, accessed July 15, 2014, http://www.age-of-the-sage.org/evolution/tiktaalik_fins _limbs_fossil.html.

18. *Outer Ear Anatomy Diagram*, art, from Medical Anatomy, December 11, 2013, http://medicalanatomy.net/outer-ear-anatomy-diagram.

19. *Illustration of von Baer's Law*, art, from Suzette F. Chopin, "Development," Biology Reference, accessed April 23, 2014, http://www.biologyreference.com/Co-Dn /Development.html.

20. *MedlinePlus*, s.v. "Fetal Development: Week by Week Changes," last modified September 30, 2013, http://www.nlm.nih.gov/medlineplus/ency/article/002398.htm.

21. Shubin, *Your Inner Fish*, 90.

22. Bjorn Carey, "Human Ears Evolved from Ancient Fish Gills," LiveScience, January 18, 2006, http://www.livescience.com/558-human-ears-evolved-ancient-fish-gills.html.

23. "Ears and Altitude," American Academy of Otolaryngology—Head and Neck Surgery, last modified February 2, 2012, http://www.entnet.org/content/ears-and -altitude.

24. "Embryos and Evolution," Evolution Matters, accessed July 18, 2014, http://www .ucsd.tv/evolutionmatters/lesson2/study.shtml.

25. "What Is a Protein?" Learn.Genetics: Genetic Science Learning Center, accessed July 16, 2014, http://learn.genetics.utah.edu/content/molecules/proteins.

26. "Homeotic Genes and Body Patterns," Learn.Genetics: Genetic Science Learning Center, accessed July 18, 2014, http://learn.genetics.utah.edu/content/variation /hoxgenes.

27. "The History of Cloning," Learn.Genetics: Genetic Science Learning Center, accessed July 18, 2014, http://learn.genetics.utah.edu/content/cloning/clonezone.

28. Helen Pearson, "Scientists Grow Bladder Replacement in Lab," *Nature*, April 4, 2006, http://www.nature.com/news/2006/060403/full/news060403-3.html.

29. Matt Kaplan, "DNA Has a 521-Year Half-Life," *Nature*, October 10, 2012, http:// www.nature.com/news/dna-has-a-521-year-half-life-1.11555.

30. Ann Gibbons, "Bonobos Join Chimps as Closest Human Relatives," *Science*, June 13, 2012, http://news.sciencemag.org/plants-animals/2012/06/bonobos-join-chimps -closest-human-relatives.

31. Michael Musso, "Human DNA Similarities to Chimps and Bananas, What Does It Mean?," *Gene Cuisine* (blog), March 4, 2011, http://genecuisine.blogspot.be/2011/03 /human-dna-similarities-to-chimps-and.html; "Genes in Common," The Tech Museum of Innovation, accessed July 31, 2014, genetics.thetech.org/online-exhibits/genes-common; Esther Inglis-Arkell, "Why Are Mushrooms More like Humans than They Are like Plants?," io9, September 7, 2012, io9.com/5940434/why-are-mushrooms-more-like -humans-than-they-are-like-plants.

32. *Genetics Home Reference*, s.v. "Retrovirus," last modified August 25, 2014, http://ghr .nlm.nih.gov/glossary=retrovirus.

33. "Three Layers of Endogenous Retroviral Evidence for the Evolutionary Model," *Evidence for the Evolutionary Model*, last modified May 2012, http://www .evolutionarymodel.com/ervs.htm.

34. Elaine A. Ostrander and Robert K. Wayne, "The Canine Genome," *Genome Research* 15 (2005): 1706–16, http://genome.cshlp.org/content/15/12/1706.full.

35. Robert Roy Britt, "Unlikely Cousins: Whales and Hippos," LiveScience, January 25, 2004, http://www.livescience.com/102-cousins-whales-hippos.html.

36. News Staff, "Indohyus: The 'Missing Link' between Whales and Four-Legged Ancestors," Science 2.0, December 20, 2007, http://www.science20.com/news_releases /indohyus_are_the_missing_link_between_whales_and_four_legged_ancestors.

37. Bjorn Carey, "Convergent Evolution in Poison Frogs," LiveScience, August 8, 2005, http://www.livescience.com/370-convergent-evolution-poison-frogs.html.

38. "Hummingbirds and Hummingbirdoid Moths," Map of Life, accessed July 18, 2014, http://www.mapoflife.org/topics/topic_121_Hummingbirds-and-hummingbirdoid -moths/.

39. "Cleaner Fish," infosources.org, accessed July 18, 2014, http://www.infosources.org /what_is/Cleaner_fish.html.

40. "The Comparative Method and the Evolution of Aposematism," The Summers Lab, accessed July 18, 2014, http://core.ecu.edu/biol/summersk/summerwebpage/topics /mimicry.html.

41. Ed Yong, "Fake Cleaner Fish Dons Multiple Disguises," *Not Exactly Rocket Science* (blog), October 24, 2009, http://scienceblogs.com/notrocketscience/2009/10/24/fake -cleaner-fish-dons-multiple-disguises.

42. "All Lives Transform," Morning Earth, accessed July 18, 2014, http://www.morning -earth.org/Graphic-E/Transf-Mimic.html; Mary Bates, "Praying Mantis Mimics Flower to Trick Prey," *National Geographic News*, September 25, 2013, http://newswatch .nationalgeographic.com/2013/09/25/praying-mantis-mimics-flower-to-trick-prey.

43. "*Gongylus gongylodes* (Violin Mantis, Indian Rose Mantis)," DeShawn's MantisKingdom.com, accessed July 18, 2014, http://mantiskingdom.com/index .php?main_page=page&id=12&chapter=1.

44. "Fossil," The Nova Scotia Legislature, accessed July 18, 2014, http://nslegislature .ca/index.php/about/symbols/fossil.

45. Helen Thompson, "Colorful Plumage Began with Feathered Dinosaurs," Smithsonian.com, February 13, 2014, http://www.smithsonianmag.com/science-nature /colorful-plumage-began-with-feathered-dinosaurs-180949691.

46. "*Estemmenosuchus mirabilis*," Science NetLinks, August 6, 2013, http://sciencenetlinks .tumblr.com/post/57534511865.

47. "*Thrinaxodon*," Prehistoric-Wildlife.com, accessed July 19, 2014, http://www .prehistoric-wildlife.com/species/t/thrinaxodon.html.

48. Alicia Chang, "New Tyrannosaur Fossil Found in China Suggests a Soft Downy Coat of Feathers," *Lakeland Ledger*, April 4, 2012, http://www.theledger.com/article /20120404/news/120409733.

49. Harold L. Levin, *The Earth through Time*, 8th ed. (New York: John Wiley & Sons, 2006), 437.

50. Charles Q. Choi, "Why Odd Egg-Laying Mammals Still Exist," LiveScience, September 21, 2009, http://www.livescience.com/5746-odd-egg-laying-mammals -exist.html.

51. Beverly Bird, "Nutritional Facts on Ostrich Eggs," Livestrong.com, last modified August 16, 2013, http://www.livestrong.com/article/345784-nutritional-facts-on -ostrich-eggs.

52. "Just about Mosasaurs," Oceans of Kansas, last modified March 4, 2011, http://oceansofkansas.com/about-mo.html.

53. John Hutchinson, "What Killed the Dinosaurs?," DinoBuzz, last modified September 28, 2005, http://www.ucmp.berkeley.edu/diapsids/extinctheory.html.

54. Wilson da Silva, "A Very Big Bang," *Cosmos*, March 23, 2011, http://wdas .cosmosmagazine.com/features/a-very-big-bang/.

10. HAS THE STORY OF EVOLUTION BEEN PROVEN FOR SURE?

1. Frank Newport, "In U.S., 46% Hold Creationist View of Human Origins," Gallup, June 1, 2012, http://www.gallup.com/poll/155003/hold-creationist-view-human -origins.aspx.

2. "Ipsos Global @dvisory: Supreme Being(s), the Afterlife and Evolution," Ipsos, April 25, 2011, http://www.ipsos-na.com/news-polls/pressrelease.aspx?id=5217.

3. Chris Kirk, "Map: Publicly Funded Schools That Are Allowed to Teach Creationism," *Slate*, January 26, 2014, http://www.slate.com/articles/health_and _science/science/2014/01/creationism_in_public_schools_mapped_where_tax_money _supports_alternatives.html.

4. Kim Ann Zimmerman, "What Is a Scientific Theory?," LiveScience, July 19, 2012, http://www.livescience.com/21491-what-is-a-scientific-theory-definition-of-theory.html.

5. William R. Miller, "Tardigrades," *American Scientist* 99, no. 5 (September–October 2011), http://www.americanscientist.org/issues/feature/tardigrades/1.

6. Space.com Staff, "Creature Survives Naked in Space," Space.com, September 8, 2008, http://www.space.com/5817-creature-survives-naked-space.html.

7. Matt Simon, "Absurd Creature of the Week: The Incredible Critter That's Tough Enough to Survive in Space," *Wired*, March 21, 2014, http://www.wired.com/2014/03/absurd-creature-week-water-bear.

8. "Missing Links," Answers in Genesis, accessed July 31, 2014, http://answersingenesis.org/missing-links; Mark Buetow, "The 'Missing Link': Still Missing the Gospel," Higher Things, accessed July 31, 2014, http://dtbl.org/2052.

9. Arallyn, post on *Biomedical Ephemera, or: A Frog for Your Boils* (blog), December 20, 2012, http://biomedicalephemera.tumblr.com/post/38393863999/skiagraphs-x-rays-of-the-hands-and-feet-of-a.

10. Nicholas Wade, "Ecuadorean Villagers May Hold Secret to Longevity," *New York Times*, February 16, 2011, http://www.nytimes.com/2011/02/17/science/17longevity.html?_r=0.

11. John Quinones, Laura Viddy, and Cecile Bouchardeau, "Real-life 'Werewolves,'" ABC News, September 12, 2007, http://abcnews.go.com/Primetime/story?id=2258069.

12. Humphrey Clarke, "How Bad Were the Mongols?," *Quodlibeta* (blog), December 13, 2011, http://bedejournal.blogspot.nl/2011/12/how-bad-were-mongols.html.

13. Hillary Mayell, "Genghis Khan a Prolific Lover, DNA Data Implies," *National Geographic News*, February 14, 2003, http://news.nationalgeographic.com/news/2003/02/0214_030214_genghis.html.

14. Karin Strohecker, "Fisheries Producing Small, Less Fertile Fish," ABC Science, November 23, 2007, http://www.abc.net.au/science/articles/2007/11/23/2099040.htm.

15. Alison Campbell, "Rapid Evolutionary Change in Lizards," *BioBlog*, May 6, 2008, http://sci.waikato.ac.nz/bioblog/2008/05/rapid-evolutionary-change-in-l.shtml.

16. Hugh Pennington, "Eight Things You Should Know about *E. Coli*," *Environmental Health News*, February 7, 2014, http://www.ehn-online.com/news/article.aspx?id=11894.

17. Bob Holmes, "Bacteria Make Major Evolutionary Shift in the Lab," *New Scientist*, June 9, 2008, http://www.newscientist.com/article/dn14094-bacteria-make-major-evolutionary-shift-in-the-lab.html.

18. Dawkins, *The Greatest Show on Earth*, 117–31.

19. "Nasty Nature: The Liver Fluke Commands You!," *The Zed Word* (blog), June 14, 2009, http://www.zedwordblog.com/2009/06/nasty-nature-liver-fluke-commands-you .html; "Liverfluke: Livestock—and Livelihoods—at Risk," Novartis Animal Health, accessed August 4, 2014, http://www.farmanimalhealth.co.uk/sheep-liver-fluke.

20. "A Man Named Charles Osborne Had Hiccups for Approximately 68 Years," SciFacts, November 27, 2010, http://www.scifacts.net/674/a_man_named_charles _osborne_had_hiccups_for_approximately_68_years.

21. C. Claiborne Ray, "Q.&.A.; Dangerous Hiccups," *New York Times*, February 22, 2000, http://www.nytimes.com/2000/02/22/science/q-a-dangerous-hiccups.html.

22. Shubin, *Your Inner Fish*, 190–222.

23. Dawkins, *The Greatest Show on Earth*, 370–71.

24. P. Z. Myers, "The Mexican Blind Cavefish Raises the Challenging Evolutionary Question: Does Disuse Lead to Degeneration or Dissappearance of a Feature? Here, an Answer Darwin Would Have Loved," *SeedMagazine.com*, January 10, 2007, http:// seedmagazine.com/content/article/pz_myers_on_how_the_cavefish_lost_its_eyes; Lisa Miller, "Why Are Cave Salamanders Blind?," PawNation, accessed July 31, 2014, http:// animals.pawnation.com/cave-salamanders-blind-1534.html.

25. Tamsin Woolley-Barker, "The Biomimicry Manual: What Can the Bombardier Beetle Teach Us about Fuel Injection?," *Inhabitat* (blog), August 28, 2013, http://inhabitat.com /the-biomimicry-manual-what-can-the-bombardier-beetle-teach-us-about-fuel-injection.

26. "Dropping a Bomb on Creationists—The Bombardier Beetle," *The Infinite Variety* (blog), March 26, 2010, http://theinfinitevariety.wordpress.com/2010/03/26/dropping -a-bomb-on-creationists-the-bombardier-beetle.

27. Imperial College London, "Will Beetles Inherit the Earth? Evolutionary Study Reveals Their Long-Term Success," ScienceDaily, December 26, 2007, http://www .sciencedaily.com/releases/2007/12/071220140810.htm.

28. "Dropping a Bomb on Creationists."

11. FROM MOUSE TO MAN

1. Dennis O'Neil, "The First Primates," Palomar College, last modified March 21, 2004, http://anthro.palomar.edu/earlyprimates/first_primates.htm.

2. University of Utah, "The Oldest Homo Sapiens: Fossils Push Human Emergence Back to 195,000 Years Ago," ScienceDaily, February 28, 2005, http://www.sciencedaily .com/releases/2005/02/050223122209.htm.

3. William L. Jungers, "Lucy's Length: Stature Reconstruction in *Australopithecus afarensis* (A.L.288–1) with Implications for Other Small-Bodied Hominids," *American Journal of Physical Anthropology* 76, no. 2 (April 27, 2005): 227–31, http://onlinelibrary .wiley.com/doi/10.1002/ajpa.1330760211/abstract;jsessionid=CEAAA5F81C7776F148 D63B032BA37944.f01t04.

4. "Lucy's Story," Arizona State University Institute of Human Origins, accessed July 18, 2014, https://iho.asu.edu/about/lucy's-story.

5. Ibid; Dawkins, *The Greatest Show on Earth*, 188–89.

6. Robin Anne Smith, "How Did Human Brains Get to Be So Big?," *Scientific American*, February 21, 2012, http://blogs.scientificamerican.com/guest-blog/2012/02/21/how-did -human-brains-get-to-be-so-big.

7. Xauri'El Zwaan, "The Link between Bipedalism and Increased Brain Size," Sciences 360, February 17, 2009, http://www.sciences360.com/index.php/the-link-between -bipedalism-and-increased-brain-size-16928.

8. Timothy Meinch, "Scientists Eager to Learn from World's Smartest Ape," *Des Moines Register*, February 1, 2014, http://www.desmoinesregister.com/story /news/2014/02/01/scientists-eager-to-learn-from-worlds-smartest-ape/5099479.

9. Paul Raffaele, "Speaking Bonobo," *Smithsonian Magazine*, November 2006, http:// www.smithsonianmag.com/science-nature/speaking-bonobo-134931541/; "Bonobo vs Pacman," YouTube video, 2:48, posted by "Stijn Vogels," October 25, 2006, https:// www.youtube.com/watch?v=Rh8gfIcjQNY.

10. Rebecca Wragg Sykes, "What Kanzi Didn't Do . . . Yet," *The Rocks Remain* (blog), August 24, 2012, http://www.therocksremain.org/2012/08/what-kanzi-didnt-doyet .html.

11. David Keys, "A Dental Clue to Life in Britain 500,000 Years Ago," *The Independent*, September 8, 1995, http://www.independent.co.uk/news/a-dental-clue-to-life-in -britain-500000-years-ago-1599961.html.

12. "*Sahelanthropus tchadensis*," Smithsonian National Museum of Natural History, accessed July 21, 2014, http://humanorigins.si.edu/evidence/human-fossils/species /sahelanthropus-tchadensis.

13. Fran Dorey and Beth Blaxland, "*Homo ergaster*," Australian Museum, last modified February 25, 2013, http://australianmuseum.net.au/Homo-ergaster.

14. "*Homo erectus*," Smithsonian National Museum of Natural History, accessed July 21, 2014, http://humanorigins.si.edu/evidence/human-fossils/species/homo-erectus.

15. *"Homo neanderthalensis,"* Smithsonian National Museum of Natural History, accessed July 21, 2014, http://humanorigins.si.edu/evidence/human-fossils/species /homo-neanderthalensis.

16. University of Utah, "The Oldest Homo Sapiens."

17. *"Homo erectus."*

18. "Tracing Fossil Finds: A Hominid Timeline," Exploratorium, accessed July 21, 2014, http://www.exploratorium.edu/evidence/lowbandwidth/INT_hominid_timeline.html.

19. "The Relationship between Modern Humans and Neanderthals," Smithsonian National Museum of Natural History, accessed July 21, 2014, http://humanorigins .si.edu/evidence/genetics/ancient-dna-and-neanderthals/interbreeding.

20. Pallab Ghosh, "Study Backs 'Hobbit' Island Dwarfism Theory," BBC News, April 16, 2013, http://www.bbc.com/news/science-environment-22166736.

21. Wynne Parry, "Age Confirmed for 'Eve,' Mother of All Humans," LiveScience, August 18, 2010, http://www.livescience.com/10015-age-confirmed-eve-mother -humans.html.

22. Nancy Atkinson, "Organics Found in Mars Meteorites, but Nothing Biological," Universe Today, June 20, 2012, http://www.universetoday.com/95892/organics-found -in-mars-meteorites-but-nothing-biological; Michael D. Lemonick, "Mars: New Clues to Life in 'Lake Doughnut,'" *Time*, December 9, 2013, http://science.time.com/2013/12/09 /mars-new-clues-to-life-in-lake-doughnut.

23. Gillie Jayne, "Could Life Survive on Europa?," *Astronomy Wise* (blog), October 6, 2013, http://www.astronomywise.com/articles/could-life-survive-on-europa; "Life As We *Didn't* Know It," NASA, accessed July 31, 2014, http://science.nasa.gov/science -news/science-at-nasa/2001/ast13apr_1.

24. *Brain Functions*, art, from The Brain Tumor Awareness Organization, accessed April 21, 2014, http://www.braintumorawareness.org/btfacts.html.

25. D. F. Swaab, *We Are Our Brains: A Neurobiography of the Brain, from the Womb to Alzheimer's* (New York: Random House, 2014), 273–303.

INDEX

Note: An *italicized* page number indicates an illustration.

A

Acanthostega, 136, 163

adaptation, 43, 51. *see also* evolution

Africa, 126, 148-149, 197, 198

amino acids, 78-80, 81, 86-87, 88-89, 91, 142-143

amphibians, 33, 124, 131-134, 137, 152, 173

ancestors, common, 37, 40, 43, 198

ancestors, human, 37, 40, 43, 119, 187-198

anglerfish, 10-11

animal breeders, 38-40

Anomalocaris, 114

ants, 65-69, 73, 109, 171-172, 202

apes, 146-147, 151, 187-188, 193. *see also* chimpanzees *and other apes*

archaea, 88, 94, 101, 108

armor, 116-117

arms, 134-136

arthropods, 116-117, 119

atmosphere, 31-32, 92, 201

atoms, 3-4, 7, 23, 28, 29

Australia, 100, 123

Australopithecus, 188

B

backbones, 118-119

bacteria, 7-11, 97, 101, 108, 109, 145, 168-170. *see also* archaea; snottites

beauty, 62

bees, 202

behaviors, 69-70, 71

belief and brain, 203-205

Bible. *see* creationism, gods and religions

Big Bang, 25, 27-28, 29

bipedality, 189-192

birds, 60, 119, 136, 141, 152. *see also* peacocks *and other birds*

blood vessels, 5

bluestriped fangblennies, 149-150

body sizes, 163, 166

bombardier beetle, 176-180

bones, 104, 119, 134-137, 187-188, 190-191

bonobos, 144, 187, 193-194. *see also* apes

bowerbirds, 56, 57-59

brains
  complexity of, 5, 7

energy and, 154-155, 192

flatworms and, 107

human, 141, 199

individual development of, 14-15

liver flukes and, 172

looking and, 106

mammals and, 156

religious belief and, 203-205

butterflies, 149

butts, 107, 108

C

cells
  cooperation and, 7
  death of, 5, 6
  differentiation of, 141-144
  division of, 12
  first, 28, 33
  number of, 4-5
  parts of, 86-88, 102
  plant and skin, 6
  proteins and, 79, 143

chalk, 125-126

chemistry, 84-85

chickadees, 152

chicken-and-egg problems, 82-83, 125-126

mutations, 109, 163

N

natural selection, 43, 53, 62-63, 111. *see also* sexual selection

nature, 12-15, 172-173

nautiloids, 116

Neanderthals, 194, 196-198

Noah's flood, 19

"normal," 165-166

North Pole, 133-134

notochords, 118

now, 126, *129*

numbers, size of, ix

O

oceans. *see also* life; seashells on mountains

550 million years ago, 111-114

human ancestors and, 117-120

jellyfish and, 104-107

most successful creature and, 114-117

mountains and, 19

multiple-celled organisms and, 103-104

oxygen and, 100-103

parents and, 108-111

single-celled organisms and, 97-100

species and, 51

where life began and, 32, 91-96

ocean to land shift, 121

On the Origin of Species (Darwin), 44-46

opabinia, 112

Osborne, Charles, 173

oxygen, 4-5, 97, 100-103, 124

P

paleontologists, 131

palm trees, 129

Panderichthys, 132

parents, 109-110, 144

peacocks, 55, 57, 59-60

periods of Earth's history, 21, *22, 125, 126, 129*, 156

planets, 28, 29-30, *31*, 97, 201. *see also* universe

plants

cells of, 6

Darwin on, 43

first, 33

fossils and, 20

land, 121

new species of, 38-39

protein and, 79

sunlight and, 100

plates, tectonic, 128

plutonium, 23

polar regions, 133-134

population control, 12, 40-41

predators, 111-114, 116, 119, 149-150, 202

prey, 10, 51-52, 55-56, 111-114, 119, 149-150

proofs of evolution. *see* evolution, proofs of

prosimians, 187

proteins

amino acids and, 79

cell communication and, 143

cells and, 79, 143

DNA and, 80-83, 86-87, 142-143

meat and, 111

oxygen and, 102

pterosaurs, 155

Pytoraptor, 152

R

rabbits, 51-52, 55, 60, 62-63

radioactivity, 23, 130

religions. *see* creationism, gods and religions

reproduction, 77, 83, 108

reptiles, 33, 119, 129, 137, 152-153, 155, 156

RNA (ribonucleic acid), *81-88*, 146

robots, 1-3, 4

rocket-building analogy, 185-187, 195

rocks, ages of, 20-23, 125-131, 132

rocks, liquid, 31

rotting, 21-22

S

sacrifice, self-, 67-68, 71, 73

Sahelanthropus tchadensis, 194

salamanders, 152, 176

salt, 84-85

sandstone, 132

When he was young, **Jan Paul Schutten** didn't know what he wanted to be when he grew up: a police officer or a cowboy? Or maybe an astronaut? When he actually grew up, he knew—he wanted to be a writer, and he has been writing children's nonfiction since 2003. A native of the Netherlands, his books are popular and critically acclaimed; he has won several awards including the Gouden Griffel (Golden Stylus) for *Children of Amsterdam* in 2008 and again for *The Mystery of Life* in 2014. *The Mystery of Life* is his second book to be translated into English. Also available in English is *Hello from 2030*.

Illustrator **Floor Rieder** loves patterns and is inspired by artists like Norman Messenger, Carson Ellis, and M.C. Escher. After attending art school where she studied illustration, she moved to Amsterdam and got her first illustrating job at the newspaper Het Parool. *The Mystery of Life* is her first children's book for which she received the illustration awards Zilveren Penseel (Silver Pencil) and Gouden Penseel (Golden Pencil). In 2014, a new edition of *Alice in Wonderland* and *Through the Looking Glass* with Floor's illustrations was published in the Netherlands.

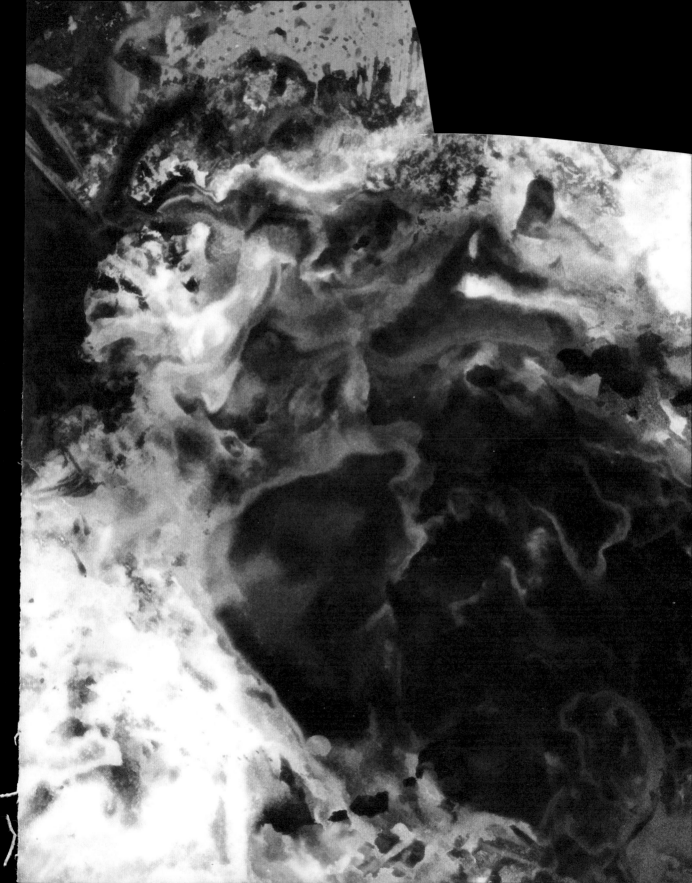

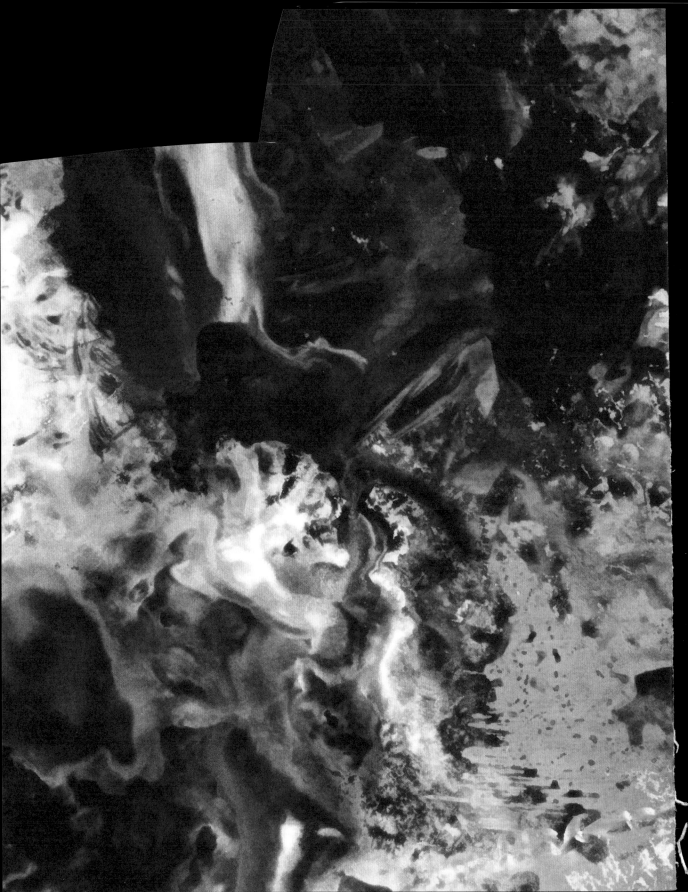